Democracy

KEY CONCEPTS

Published

Colin Barnes and Geof Mercer, *Disability*
Steve Bruce, *Fundamentalism*
Anthony Elliott, *Concepts of the Self*
Michael Freeman, *Human Rights*
Michael Saward, *Democracy*
John Scott, *Power*
Anthony D. Smith, *Nationalism: Theory, Ideology, History*

Forthcoming

Barbara Adam, *Time*
Martin Albrow, *Globalization*
Alan Aldridge, *Consumption*
Darin Barney, *The Network Society*
Mildred Blaxter, *Health*
Harriet Bradley, *Gender*
Michael Harry Brighouse, *Justice*
Craig Calhoun, *Community*
Francis G. Castles, *Welfare and the Welfare State*
David Coates, *Capitalism*
Keith Dowding, *Rational Choice*
Tim Dunne, *International Society*
Katrin Flikschuh, *Freedom*
John P. S. Gearson, *Terrorism*
Keith Grint, *Work*
Russell Hardin, *Trust*
Fred Inglis, *Culture*
Robert H. Jackson, *Sovereignty: The Evolution of an Idea*
Peter Jones, *Toleration*
Mette Kjaer, *Governance*
Keith Krause and Michael C. Williams, *Security*
Ruth Lister, *Poverty*
Jon Mandle, *Global Justice*
Anthony Payne and Nicola Phillips, *Development*
Judith Philips, *Care*
Chris Phillipson, *Ageing*
Raymond Plant and Selina Siong-Li Chen, *Citizenship*
Kenneth Prandy, *Social Mobility*
Jennifer Jackson Preece, *Minority Rights*
John Toye, *Development*
Stuart White, *Equality*

Democracy

Michael Saward

polity

First published in 2003 by Polity Press in association with Blackwell Publishing Ltd

Editorial office:
Polity Press
65 Bridge Street
Cambridge CB2 1UR, UK

Marketing and production:
Blackwell Publishing Ltd
108 Cowley Road
Oxford OX4 1JF, UK

Distributed in the USA by
Blackwell Publishing Inc.
350 Main Street
Malden, MA 02148, USA

A catalogue record for this book is available from the British Library.

Library of Congress Cataloging-in-Publication Data
Saward, Michael, 1960–
    Democracy / Michael Saward.
p. cm. – (Key concepts)
    Includes bibliographical references and index.
    ISBN 0-7456-2349-2 – ISBN 0-7456-2350-6 (pbk.)
    1. Democracy. I. Title. II. Series: Key concepts (Polity Press)
JC423.S27478 2003
321.8—dc21

2002012194

Typeset in 10½ on 12 pt Sabon
by SNP Best-set Typesetter Ltd., Hong Kong
Printed and bound in Great Britain by MPG Books Ltd, Bodmin, Cornwall

For further information on Polity, visit our website:
http://www.polity.co.uk

Contents

Introduction   vii

1   Is *This* Democracy?   1

2   Narrating Democracy I   32

3   Narrating Democracy II   58

4   Five Challenges   84

5   Reinventing Democracy   116

Conclusion   140

Glossary: Conceptions of Democracy   144

A Guide to Further Reading   152

Notes   158

Bibliography   161

Index   169

For Nadia, Zachary and Iman

Introduction

'Democracy' is a powerful political weapon. Wars are fought and justified in its name; the post-September 11, 2001, 'war on terror' is no exception. Even leaders on the political extremes claim it for their actions. Democracy seems to be an idea and a practice at the heart of modern politics, all over the world. But with importance comes familiarity, and 'democracy' as a word is so familiar that we often do not bother to ask – what is it? Many people – not least politicians, university academics and journalists – think they know the answers. But disagreement is rife. And, oddly enough, it may be the depth of disagreements about 'democracy' that make it so powerful, so important. A word *that* versatile can make a powerful tool or weapon for use by a great many people in different ways.

In this book I start and finish with the disagreements. On one level, you could even say that democracy *is* the contest over its meaning. If democracy were a building, the 'under construction' sign would never be removed. Architects would squabble over the right design. Builders would argue over the appropriate materials. Others would fight over who really owned it, where it should be built, who should live in it and who should be kept out. One could observe all this and have two very different reactions – despair because the right way to build a democracy will never be discovered if argument continues, or fascination at the twists and turns and possibilities of the arguments. This book is a product of something like the second reaction. It is about the idea of democracy, about aspects of how that idea is constructed, contested, fought over, implemented, revised. Many models of democracy are discussed, but no single model or design is put across as the 'right' one or regarded as a finished, pristine product. I try to capture and describe some of the materials and actions and words of those who construct ideas of democracy – from political leaders to ordinary citizens to academic theorists – along with the dilemmas that prompt their efforts and challenges they must face.

In the chapters that follow, the idea of democracy is explored in different ways. On the one hand, I 'step' from case studies to generalizations and back, and from theory to practice and back; on the other, I 'dip' selectively into cases and texts and debates. These strategies are used to sketch debates, not to provide the full picture (even if that were possible). The guide to further reading at the end of the book will suggest other places where readers can look for more depth on particular topics.

Instances of the 'stepping' and 'dipping' strategies can be found in all chapters. Sometimes I look at examples of argument about 'democracy' from recent events in specific countries, and ask what democracy means to different political actors and what it might mean to us. In chapter 1 in particular I examine a range of cases – from General Musharraf's coup in Pakistan in 1999 and his referendum in 2002, to the US presidential election deadlock in Florida in 2000, to anti-European propaganda in the United Kingdom in 2001 – to search for answers to the question 'what is democracy?' At other times I use hypothetical examples in order to try to tease out our intuitions about what it might mean to 'design' a democracy; in chapter 1 I invite readers to consider the dilemmas of establishing democracy for 'country X'. I also offer close examination of particular claims and texts in order to explore interesting gaps and assumptions about democracy – for example, in a recent article by the prominent English historian Eric Hobsbawm, assumptions about what makes democracy valuable, and what threatens it.

Exploring cases and events can tell us a great deal about common and uncommon assumptions about democracy (and can force us to test our own thoughts on the matter). However, I also focus on certain *narratives* of democracy. In the realm of political ideas, and certainly in standard textbooks on the subject, certain *stories* are often told about democracy which construct it in different, often competing, ways. These narratives are important background material to our gaining an understanding of democracy, and for thinking through what is really important – for example, participation in politics by ordinary people? Occasional voting for good leaders? Regarding ourselves as the same, or respecting each others' differences? In chapters 2 and 3, I offer an overview of dominant and challenging narratives of democracy from approximately the past 150 years. The foundation of these narratives lies in the work of some prominent *theorists* of democracy – we shall encounter diverse figures such as James Madison, Jeremy Bentham, Joseph Schumpeter, Antonio Gramsci and Robert A. Dahl. Sometimes I focus in closely on particular arguments in single works which have been influential in putting across a certain idea of democracy. At other times I step back in order to adopt a more panoramic perspective. Well-established narratives of democracy are historical products of the efforts of different writers and advocates at different times, the unintended and unfinished product of many hands. They can help us to understand what is at stake in real-world debates, and to see how things connect (how, for instance, interpreting *human nature* one way can lead to thinking of *democracy* in a particular, compatible, way).

These narratives of democracy may seem to have a beginning and an end, like a conventional story. But no interpretation of democracy can be sealed off from new and persistent *challenges* to its assumptions and assertions. In chapter 4 I explore the character and importance of a selected, diverse set of challenges to democracy today. It could be said that models of democracy which cannot adapt successfully in the face of these challenges will be so much the worse for that failure. I offer thoughts on globalization, environmentalism, complexity, cultural diversity, and measuring democracy, setting out how developments under these headings pose direct challenges to long-held and central assumptions about democracy, and politics.

Finally, chapter 5 considers the fertile wave of thinking and writing about democracy in the past ten to fifteen years, including new or revived deliberative, cosmopolitan, ecological and associative models, along with efforts to revive the ancient ideal of direct democracy. Like the discussion of the narratives of democracy in chapters 2 and 3, these approaches offer partial stories about what democracy can and should mean, how it can and should be practised, how it might be *reinvented*. Although no artificial, one-to-one correspondence is attempted, some of these new recent approaches have arisen in part as responses to the challenges discussed in chapter 4. Ecological approaches to democracy – or revisions of democracy – arise in response to the emergence of the environmentalists' challenges to orthodox representative politics, and cosmopolitan approaches are offered as one way of dealing with many of the developments that are lumped together under the broad term 'globalization'.

Overall, each of these approaches – case studies, texts, narratives, diverse challenges, revisions – to examining the idea of democracy has value. At least, I hope to show that is the case. But none is enough on its own, or obviously more valuable than the others. Dipping into real-world events and arguments is vital if we are to see how democracy is disputed, for example, but that alone is not enough. We also need to step back from the messiness of daily political life to gain broader perspectives. Stepping back and forward between theory and practice, for example, has a great deal to recommend it – at best, we don't get bogged down in particular times and places, and neither do we indulge in mere 'armchair theory', divorced from real political dilemmas affecting real people. So, the book hopes to show by example how an eclectic mix of approaches can enrich our appreciation of social ideas.

Finally, it is important to note that my aim in this book is to provoke thought about the meaning, value and possibilities of democracy. I offer a starting point for debating and analysing democracy, not a blueprint. No particular line on the subject is pushed, no theory strongly favoured. The approach adopted is based on the conviction that undergraduate students (and others) need to be prompted to think about *their* responses to 'democracy' as a word, an idea and a practice. Many classical, modern and contemporary ideas about democracy are discussed, but the intention throughout is to guide rather than to tell, to tease out and explore possible meanings rather than to prescribe them.

Chapter 5 includes material from my article 'Reconstructing Democracy' which appeared in the journal *Government and Opposition* in 2001. I wish to thank the editor for his kind permission to use it here.

Michael Saward

1

Is *This* Democracy?

Introduction

'Democracy' can be found in familiar and unfamiliar practices, predictable and surprising contexts. This chapter dips into some such practices, contexts. It contains (a) three real-world case studies of political voices from Pakistan, the USA and the UK, (b) a hypothetical case study of 'country X', and (c) close reading of texts arguing for democracy's worth and its limits. My aim is to provoke a set of questions about democracy's meaning and value which arise from our searches. My conviction is that attention to democracy's detailed texture can make us think in fresh ways about the subject. If the conviction is right and the aim achieved, we can move on armed with a creative sense of democracy's multi-sidedness and its perplexities, all the better to deal with the narratives, challenges and revisions that form the focus of later chapters.

Let me start with a little jargon that will help guide us through the explorations in this opening chapter. Literary and cultural theorists often talk about words (and pictures and events and objects) as *signifiers* – they suggest or provoke or signify certain thoughts, ideas and concepts (which we can call the *signifieds*). For example, the word 'police' is a signifier; what it signifies might be someone in a certain uniform, or the idea of 'law and order' maybe. Looked at another way, what 'police' signifies could be a person and a thing (someone in uniform), or another abstract idea (law and order), or something else again. Some words signify in quite stable and straightforward ways – we might all agree pretty much what they refer to, such as 'bicycle', for example. Political terms are renowned for their *unstable* nature as signifiers. Even seemingly innocuous phrases such as 'the Oval Office' might signify a diverse range of things – authority, deception, patriotism, secrecy, American democracy, American colonialism, strong leadership, history and continuity, and so on.

This chapter is about 'democracy' as a signifier. What does this word suggest, convey, evoke? (What does it signify for *you*?) How do politicians and political scientists and ordinary people use it? What work does it do in different contexts? What meanings are constructed for it? And how can we know which meanings, if any, are the 'real' ones?

Making and using 'democracy': three contexts

A great many things are done in the name of democracy. Decisions are taken, institutions created and destroyed, wars fought. Governments, dissidents and dictators all claim it for their actions. In order to praise or criticize, or extend or contract, what may be done in the name of democracy, politicians and others attempt to 'fix' the meaning of the word when they use it. They try to attach a particular 'signified' to the word, to mould it to their purposes. We are now going to look at three quite specific examples of such attempts. Each case will provoke some awkward questions about what we and others think democracy is. In a moment we will take a critical look at how the experts, such as political theorists, define democracy; before that, it is important that we explore our own responses and intuitions.

Justifying the general's coup: Pakistan after October 1999

First, let us look at some recent events in Pakistan, a country that has had unhappy experience of often ineffective and corrupt elected governments interspersed with military coups and military governments since it was created in 1949 out of what was colonial India. Days after leading the successful military coup in Pakistan in October 1999 which overthrew the elected government of Prime Minister Nawaz Sharif, General Pervez Musharraf declared that he was instituting:

> not martial law, only another path towards democracy. The armed forces have no intention to stay in charge any longer than is absolutely necessary to pave the way for true democracy to flourish in Pakistan.

He went on:

> what Pakistan has experienced in recent years has merely been a label of democracy, not the essence of it. Our people were never emancipated from the yoke of despotism. I shall not allow the people to be taken back to the era of sham democracy but to a true one. (Quoted in Goldenberg 1999)

What can we learn from this event and its leader's view of it? First, it is clear that to attach the word 'democracy' to one's actions is clearly seen as an advantage; it seems to be a way of *commending* the action simply by *describing* it. Invoking democracy, it is assumed, gives credibility or legitimacy to the staging of the coup. Normally we would not think of a military overthrow of an elected civilian government as even a remote candidate for 'democratic' status; despite this, the general clearly believes strongly in the legitimacy-conferring capacity of the word, and he makes a point of claiming it for his actions.

Notice, next, that the general is keen to attach prefixes to democracy in order to make it signify what he wants. What came before was 'sham' democracy; what he is laying the ground for is 'true' democracy. On the one side there is the 'label', on the other the 'essence' of democracy. Musharraf's rhetorical strategy is simple dualism – democracy divides into just two types (sham and true), one of which is not genuine and is represented by his opponents (the sham), while the other is genuine and is represented by himself (the true). He does more than just evoke and deploy democracy as a weapon in his battle; he wants democracy to have the meaning that suits his purposes. In other words, *to evoke democracy can at the same time be to attempt to fix a (favourable) meaning to it*; to use it is, in a sense, to construct or create it anew.

I say 'normally' a military overthrow of an elected government would not be seen as a serious candidate for 'democratic' status. But is it the case that it could never be? This begs the question: what *is* the boundary of the reasonable interpretation of 'democracy'? How can we decide – can we decide – what is 'in' and what is 'out'? At what point precisely do claims to democracy become unacceptable, or plain wrong, in this and other cases? And according to *whose standards or criteria*? Would we be prepared to consider, in this case, that the coup could represent genuinely one step back to take two forward ('another path to democracy') in the context of a corrupt and inefficient civilian government? (The question of whether democracy, as a 'Western' concept, can apply in 'non-Western' contexts is taken up in chapter 4.)

Further, note that democracy is evoked here in a *particular* context. The newspaper report from which these quotes were drawn claims that the general's speech 'was tilted heavily towards a domestic audience that is hungry for a better economic future and longing to punish corrupt political leaders'. *Local* circumstances can and do dictate how certain ways of invoking democracy will be received; local language, history, knowledge, levels of trust, religion and other cultural factors condition and shape how 'democracy' conveys meaning, how it works *there*. Democracy is always democracy *somewhere*, for a certain group of people. Evoking the interests of 'the people', General Musharraf is addressing the people *of Pakistan* above all.

Certain events since 1999 make this case arguably even more interesting, even before Musharraf's central role in the 'war on terror' after September 11, 2001. First, interviewed in May 2001, the general, now 'chief executive' and soon to take on the title of president of his country, was adding detail to his earlier rhetoric about democracy. First, a rolling series of *local* elections, the first since 1987, had been instituted. With six out of twenty-one seats on all local councils reserved for women candidates, the administration, wrote the UK

journalist of *The Guardian*, was 'giving women a rare access
to power' (McCarthy 2001). The general himself claimed that
devolution of power to local and provincial units was 'real
democracy': 'We are introducing democracy to Pakistan, real
democracy at the grassroots level.' He went on to assert that
'There has never been democracy in Pakistan, real democracy,
because democracy is certainly not having elected governments . . . The more important is how an elected government
behaves, whether it is democratic in its dispensation.' Further,
he denied that personal or narrow political interest was
driving his actions: 'I didn't take power, power was thrust on
me. But I think as it stands with hindsight it was good for
Pakistan that this happened.'[1]

Second, a referendum was held in Pakistan on 30 April
2002 on whether President Musharraf should have five
further years in power, despite sticking to his promise to hold
new parliamentary elections later in 2002. After September
11, Musharraf had become a key player in the US-led
'coalition' against 'terror', since the Taliban and al-Qaeda
in neighbouring Afghanistan became the first US military
target (the swift overthrow of the Taliban government
relieved some domestic pressure on Musharraf arising from
considerable dislike and distrust of American motives among
Pakistanis). Here was a military leader, called upon by other
countries to 'restore democracy' (before the geopolitical
terrain shifted, at any rate), deploying the most democratic
of mechanisms, the referendum, which is a direct and decisive vote by the people.

Many reports noted that the general sought legitimacy for
his rule, that like all dictators he found it hard to think of
relinquishing power, and that by using a democratic mechanism he was merely underlining his lack of democratic legitimacy. Yet the president's claim was that he 'was seeking
people's opinion in a democratic way': 'People can vote in my
favour or vice versa. So this is not for me but on the issue
which needs to be decided by the people of Pakistan.'[2] In his
referendum campaign, the president sought to underline the
democratic progress made under his leadership by meeting
representatives of local government.[3] His reforms, mentioned
above, had resulted in 'thousands of councillors, including
for the first time significant numbers of women, [being]

elected to new posts' (McCarthy 2002). Musharraf said: 'they are the asset of this country and all hopes for a genuine democracy lie with them.'[4]

Of course, my aim here is not to give anything like a full factual account of these events, or to come to any immediate evaluation of the merits of the case. But taking the general's claims at face value, what do you make of them? Voting rights and guaranteed representation for women, instituting fairly elected local government units, devolving power from the centre, asserting the national or general interest, using a direct democratic device to seek people's endorsement of his rule – are these not actions with strong 'democratic' overtones? And how strong is the claim that elections are *not* crucial to democracy, but rather what matters is a leader's *behaviour*?

That example has provoked a range of conjectures and questions for us. In particular, we have conjectured that to invoke 'democracy' is to say: 'this is a good thing, a good action', and that actors will attempt to 'fix' or construct democracy's meaning in a way that suits them. We also have key questions: are there criteria for democracy, and who supplies them? What specific institutions count as democratic? And – is democracy about serving interests, such as national interests, above all else? These are difficult, provocative issues. Experts on democracy have long debated them, as we shall see as we go through the book. But let us for the moment continue with a second case – this time looking at various views of democracy from a variety of ordinary people in connection with one specific event.

Responding to Florida: the US presidential elections in 2000

The USA, of course, is commonly regarded as a democracy. Certainly the idea of democracy, and a range of institutions and practices associated with democracy, are strongly connected to the basic character of the country in the minds of US citizens. My focus here, very specifically, is on the dramatic conclusion to the story of the US presidential elections in 2000.

We will need to fill in a little background information. The USA has an electoral college system. This means that, in literal terms, when voters vote in presidential elections, they vote not (for example) for Bush or Gore or Nader, but for members of the college associated with these candidates. When elected, the latter go on to vote in turn in the electoral college some weeks later. Further, college members are elected to the college from *states*; in most states in the US federal political system, even a narrow win over other candidates in terms of the percentage of votes gained means that the winning presidential candidate gets *all* of the electoral college votes for that state. This means, among other things, that it is perfectly possible for one candidate to get more popular votes nationally but still lose the presidency on account of having fewer electoral college votes.

In the state of Florida in November 2000, US democracy came into an especially sharp, critical focus. Republican George W. Bush and Democrat Al Gore were locked into an extraordinarily close electoral battle for the state. The stakes could hardly be higher: the winner in Florida would take all of the state's electoral college votes and with them the presidency itself. Arguments raged in the courts, in the streets, in the corridors of power and in TV studios over, for example, whether all Floridians had had an equal opportunity to vote; and whether machine-counted votes had correctly been counted, or whether they should be hand-counted. Fundamental features of electoral fairness were argued openly and in detail.

The Florida poll and its aftermath have raised troubling questions about fairness and equality, starting with access to voting (black voters in particular claiming discrimination) and clarity of voting (allegedly confusing ballot papers that resulted in many claiming to have voted mistakenly), through to higher-level questioning of the role of state courts and the Supreme Court. Indeed, if one looked at the Florida vote as if one were looking at a newly democratizing 'third world' country, one might have significant questions about whether, in this instance, the USA fully qualifies as a 'democracy'. These are critical issues, to be sure, but my intentions here are not full coverage and so are much more focused. I want to explore how 'democracy', the word and the idea, were

used by an assortment of people (as weapons, as justifications, etc.) in the heat of the Florida debate.

Amid the arguments, over two weeks into the Florida
deadlock and with no resolution immediately in sight, the
BBC News website asked: 'US elections: is this democracy?'
An odd question, you might think – aren't elections the
core of democracy? A number of people felt that they had
an answer to the question. Let me stress that I do not take
the respondents' words below as correct statements about
Florida or US politics; our interest here is in the ways in which
the statements illustrate how democracy's meaning is understood and contested, the ways in which the idea figures in
people's thinking.

Joe from Philadelphia thought the 'whole process' was
'certainly not democratic'. This was because 'We've apparently sold democracy to moneyed interests who put on banal
spectacles and little else. Now we've got to face the sad truth
that our election results are probably as contrived as the
debates and everything else connected with American politics.' Musa, a Gambian in the UK, also worried about 'the
role of corporate money and political lobbyists'; 'in America
as in the UK, the people's choice does not always determine
the leader in power, and that to any reasonably minded
person is not democracy.' The question we might take from
these responses is: to what extent does 'democracy' depend
on how strings are pulled in selecting candidates or running
campaigns – rather than elections merely *happening*? If
money can buy political influence, does that make elections
undemocratic, or less genuinely democratic? How much
money, in whose hands, used how? Do elections need a 'level
playing field', a considerable degree of social and economic
equality, before we can really call them democratic?

Neville in London worried about democracy from another
angle, asking: 'How low does the electoral turnout have to
go before the system loses all democratic accountability?' It
is all very well counting, and arguing about recounting, votes
in Florida, but is it democracy if fewer than half of the electorate voted in the first place? Majority rule? Okay, but a
majority of what, of how many? But Teresa in California
protests: 'I don't see what all the fuss is about. Let DEMOC-
RACY take its course. Let the system do what it legally and

rightfully has to do to determine who will be our next president.' Maybe moneyed influence and low turnout matter less to democracy than the immediate, tangible process of voting, counting, and confirming victory according to *this* system, *our* legal rules? Then again, what sorts of rules count as democratic – given that there is huge variety in different systems?

Michael from Canada thought it was 'time to abolish the electoral college'. One criticism aimed at it (in this debate and otherwise) is that it favours states rather than national majorities. But others, such as Faye, from the USA, protest: 'this is democracy in action. We are the United STATES of America.' Our Pakistan example alerted us to the importance of thinking of the *particular* meanings and reception and history of 'democracy'. Can democracy rightly be evoked by federalists and non-federalists, centralists and decentralists? Can it, does it, *mean* on one side or the other of *this* dispute?

A further concern, from Paul in London, was that talk about electoral colleges and systems and ballot papers and vote-counting was missing the point: 'Democracy is about people making decisions having been presented with honest choices. The near-universal problem in developed "democracies" is the appalling state of the mass media. For the most part, news priorities are set by self-interested proprietors answering the demands of advertisers. News values are regularly determined by rating wars rather than the public interest.' Is democracy less about elections than about quality of media discussion and information? And, if so, to what extent?

What does democracy mean? Whatever the merits of their particular factual arguments, were these respondents on Florida 2000 *wrong* to evoke 'democracy' in their quite different ways? We do not have to listen to many of these voices to be creatively confused at the comment of 'A' from the UK that: 'If this is democracy, then maybe the Americans should start to consider if they've ever understood the word democracy.' The fact that 'A' assumes confidently that we will know what he or she means is as interesting as the fact – or I take it to be a fact – that really we can only guess at his or her meaning. What could be as powerful as a word that can, seemingly, mean one and many things at the same time?

Democracy and identity: the British Democracy Campaign

We have found various conjectures and raised a number of questions about democracy's meaning from two specific cases. Let's look at one more, and then take a step back from the detail to think about definitions of democracy.

For the Florida case, the BBC asked: 'is this democracy?' The same question is asked in our final case – this time a full-page advertisement in May 2001 from the small lobby group the British Democracy Campaign. First, a little context (though, again, detailed facts are less important here than exploring what 'democracy' signifies in these cases). In the United Kingdom, the nature and legitimacy of the country's ties to the European Union (previously European Community) since it joined in 1972 have been highly controversial politically. In the general election campaign of 2001, the context for our present case, the opposition Conservative Party was generally sceptical about 'Europe'. Specifically, it was opposed in principle to replacing the UK currency, the pound, with the new European currency, the euro (eight days before the 2001 vote, Conservatives told British voters:'you have eight days to save the pound'; seven days before . . .). The governing Labour Party had promised a referendum on the issue of the adoption of the euro (the 'single currency'), and in principle favoured joining if it judged that the circumstances were right for the country. Informally, various figures in both of these major parties more strongly opposed even continuing membership of the EU. The British Democracy Campaign – not a politically significant group in itself – was one of a number of small parties and groups opposed to continued membership.

In the advertisement, under the heading 'European Union?', we were told: '71% of British voters want a referendum on our continued membership of the European Union. 52% want to leave the EU now.' The campaign, apparently, commissioned polls which generated these figures. Then we were told: '90% of MPs, including their leaders, will not tell you where they stand' – because they did not respond, apparently, to a letter from the campaign asking them to 'support the majority British view and back the call for a free and fair referendum in the next Parliament'. After a long list of MPs who 'failed to respond', we were told that 'These MPs want your vote in the election but will not give you a vote on who should govern Britain after the election.' And then: 'Is this democracy? . . . Let the people decide.'

Clearly, again, 'democracy' is taken by the proponents of this anti-EU stance to be a powerful, legitimizing term. By asking 'is this democracy?', they are in effect asking 'is this right?', thus associating political rightness with democracy. They feel that they can call on another view of democracy – 'letting the people decide' – since their own polling makes them confident that the outcome they regard as right, politically, would ensue in a vote of the people on the issue of 'our continued membership of the European Union'. Presumably, democracy as letting the people decide might be in tension with democracy as doing what (they think) is politically right if their polls had turned out differently? 'Democracy' here is also associated both with 'the people' and 'the right result'. Although the phrase suggests all of the people, it appears to boil down to a majority of the people – suggesting perhaps that just over half of the people can speak for the whole.

Further levels of signification are interesting in this example. Note that 'democracy' appears to signify an anti-EU position generally – 'These MPs want your vote in the election but will not give you a vote on who should govern Britain after the election' – quite *apart* from what any particular vote in the UK might produce. Is democracy about which bunch of people *makes up* the group to vote, and to be governed, as well as (or rather than) the groups/countries we *currently* have going about their voting? In other words, the suggestion here is that 'democracy' is about the *constitution* of the system itself, as well as what happens *within* the system – in-system and out-system dimensions, you might say. Associated with this is the idea that the EU is by definition non-democratic – this is a campaign to rescue 'British democracy' as the proponents see it. Again, we see here the role of local evocation and signification, the attachment of local particularity to the master term in an effort to 'fix' or construct it in a particular way, and to make it useful by conveying meanings helpful to the speaker or writer.

Finally, note the device championed by this campaign – the referendum. Like General Musharraf in Pakistan, as discussed above, the campaign found the referendum to be a useful democratic trump card (in its eyes at least). As we saw, a referendum is a device for *direct* democracy, as opposed to indirect or *representative* democracy. Depending on how it is used, it can be a means for 'the people' deciding issues directly rather than having their views mediated by political representatives or others. The suggestion here is that holding a referendum is more democratic than representatives deciding – or, as they are painted here, as failing to engage with the issue at all. Could 'democracy' really mean the people *actually* deciding issues for themselves? (In chapter 5 we will look at recent advocacy of direct democracy.)

True, this is a very specific example from a rather obscure group in UK politics, the accuracy of whose claims in the advertisement were queried by many when it appeared in the press. But again we have uncovered a range of conjectures and questions to ponder.

What can democracy signify? Collecting examples together

Let us pause to gather some thoughts from our disparate examples, first by gathering some of the significations of democracy they threw up, and then by looking at some broader, troubling questions they prompted. After that I propose to look at some dictionary definitions.

First, a basic distinction might help as we move forward. The meanings of democracy arising from our three cases are *connotations* – things that 'democracy' might suggest to people, even perhaps quite obscure or unexpected things. Connotations differ from *denotations*, which are precise and direct dictionary-style definitions. Both are 'signifieds', just different sorts. Often, we rely on the clarity of denotation to guide us through the (sometime) confusion of connotation. Thus, we might weigh how useful five friends' definitions of 'democracy' are by comparing them with the one provided by (e.g.) the *Oxford English Dictionary*, using the latter as the 'authority'. But, on the other hand, who is to say what a term connotes cannot legitimately undermine or challenge what it denotes?[5]

With that distinction in mind, let's return briefly to our cases and reflect upon what they offered us. On one side, we have the issue of what 'democracy' signifies – or, what users may *want* or need it to signify in order to justify or further their own cause. Here, much depends on how receptive particular audiences might be to efforts to construct democracy's meaning in particular ways. On the other, and often closely linked, is the range of important, challenging conjectures and questions about the character of democracy that these examples have thrown up. The cases have certainly revealed a wide array of potential signifieds for democracy. There are different ways to interpret these cases; I do not claim a definitive list. 'Democracy' signifies:

- a good, moral political system
- the best available political system
- acting in the national interest
- a deception, or a ruse, to fool people ('sham')
- 'what must be right [to do]'
- 'what I/we think is right [to do]'
- counting votes
- votes counting
- the proper or appropriate level of voter turnout
- what must be done politically
- opposing special or unfairly favoured interests
- the choice of the people prevailing indirectly [normally for candidates]
- the choice of the people prevailing directly [normally for policies]
- localism, assertion of [authentic] local identity
- collective self-government by a people
- agenda-setting not unduly influenced by commercial considerations
- the voice of the people
- due process (proper procedures being followed)
- the will of the majority
- how we do it politically *here*, in this place, with these historical rules.

Slightly less directly but no less pressing have been critical and challenging questions arising from the focused Pakistani, US and UK cases, to which we will need to return later.

* Is democracy really several 'democracies', with its real meaning (if there is such a thing) being local and particular? Are there boundaries to its reasonable interpretation, and are there objective grounds for making these judgements?
* What mix of institutions, and what formal and informal processes, make up democracy? Are elections *most* fundamental?
* Is there a 'democratic' way to constitute the political unit which defines the country or other community which is to be governed?

However one might comment on the list and the questions, one key point is that there is no simple or stable signifier–signified relationship when it comes to democracy and its potential meanings. 'Democracy' is an enormously rich, suggestive, evocative political term, and it is partly this fact that makes it such a potent political weapon. We can expect that it will mean different things – perhaps very different things – to various groups and individuals. We might miss much of democracy's power and richness as a concept if we try too soon to tie down its meaning to a single institution or principle or practice. General, one-size-fits-all definitions can easily unravel when confronted with the real world of democracy.

That said, there is no shortage of neat, short, seemingly authoritative definitions of democracy available, in both dictionaries and the professional political science literature. These provide denotations of democracy; maybe they can help us to escape the play of connotation which threatens to overwhelm us? Let us look at a sample of such definitions.

Sampling professional definitions

There is a great deal of further work we can do with the list of possible signifieds, and with the key questions, that arise from our cases. Much of that work will be done in the following chapters. I *do* take the view that democracy's plenitude of potential meaning is not a licence to grant to it *whatever* meaning we might wish; some possible meanings for democracy are more reasonable than others. Chapters 2 and 3, covering influential contemporary narratives on democracy, will discuss a range of perspectives on what really counts, and what is less important, to democracy. Chapter 4 includes a discussion of possible criteria for democracy, and I refer back explicitly to the cases discussed above to argue that certain distinctions ought to be made.

In this chapter, however, my concern remains to explore a range of thoughts, and to question open-mindedly our own intuitions and prejudices about democracy's meaning and value, and to do this without stipulating or even arguing for a 'correct' definition. We turn now to a selection of definitions of democracy that have been offered by others. Which ones seem better, and (most importantly) why? What further reflections on the above cases do they prompt? Following that, we will confront the need to make choices with regard to the challenging issues and questions arising from the cases by working through a hypothetical thought experiment, in the hope that we might translate our concerns about democracy's significations into practical, or institutional, effect.

One might imagine that if we turn away from specific instances or cases of the evocation of 'democracy', and look instead at general and abstract definitions, we might get to the *essence* of our concept without the distraction of accident, argument and particularity, without prompting a further range of awkward questions to address. The chaos of connotation could be stilled, and the term could denote something clear and straightforward. However, the sorts of conjectures and questions that have arisen from the case studies can serve to disrupt seemingly clear and precise dictionary or other definitions; further connotation always lurks, disruptively, around neat definitions. But let's look at our selection and see what we can make of them.

1 'Government by the people; that form of government in which the sovereign power resides in the people as a whole, and is exercised either directly by them (as in the

small republics of antiquity) or by officers elected by them. In modern use often more vaguely denoting a social state in which all have equal rights, without hereditary or arbitrary differences of rank or privilege'; '(b) A state or community in which government is vested in the people as a whole.'

2   'A democracy is . . . a political system of which it can be said that the whole people, positively or negatively, make, and are entitled to make, the basic determining decisions on important matters of public policy.'

3   ' "Democracy" is government elected by the people.'

4   '[Democracy is] exactly what the word means etymologically – rule by the demos, the people: the people themselves make the decisions.'

5   'Basically democracy is government by discussion as opposed to government by force, and by discussion between the people or their chosen representatives as opposed to a hereditary clique. Under the tribal system whether there was a chief or not, African society was a society of equals, and it conducted its business by discussion.'

6   'a "democratic regime" is taken to mean first and foremost a set of procedural rules for arriving at collective decisions in a way which accommodates and facilitates the fullest possible participation of interested parties.'

Critically appraising the definitions

Let me start with the first definition, which is from the *Oxford English Dictionary*.[6]

'Government by the people' – immediately two issues are raised. First, again, who are 'the people'? The people of Florida, for example, or the USA, or both; of the UK, the EU, or both (or neither)? Second, is it *all* the people? What if they disagree on key issues? Can a majority speak for all? If so, what about the rights of minorities?

The definition does give us an elaboration on 'government by the people': that form of government in which the sovereign power resides in the people as a whole, and is exercised either directly by them (as in the small republics of antiquity) or by officers elected by them. If 'sovereign power' resides in the people as a whole, we will need to know what 'sovereign' means – 'ultimate', or 'final', seems likely. But we get little help on the majority/minority question – 'as a whole' just begs it once more.

But we do find the distinction familiar from textbooks on democracy – direct democracy and representative democracy. The former, the definition tells us, belongs to the long-departed habits of antiquity, the latter (presumably) common since then, and up to today.

So, interestingly, our reflections on three very specific cases earlier prompted similar questions to those we are compelled to ask of the *OED*'s efforts, too – about the political unit, for example, and about institutional mixes for democracy (direct, representative, etc.). But what can we make of our sample otherwise? (Which do you think makes a good definition, and why?)

I make four brief observations. First, regarding *strategies*, I would point out that three of these definitions stress a mechanism as the core of democracy, while three others stress a principle. In the former group are (3), which highlights the mechanism of elections, and (5) and (6), which underline discussion and procedural rules respectively. The other definitions appear to lay more emphasis on the principle that the people as a whole are entitled to make decisions, to rule, to be sovereign. I have set out in this chapter to be non-judgemental, but I will suggest that definitions based on principles may be easier to defend. What if the mechanism at the core of the first set is not the mechanism that delivers popular power? What if discussion does not work, or if elections are too infrequent and indecisive, or the procedural rules prove to be inadequate? Defining democracy in terms of principles – popular power, for example – leaves open what mix of mechanisms might best *deliver* on the principle.

Second, note that in terms of *focus*, and in the light of our earlier case discussions, certain things are absent from this selection of definitions. Absences include possible features such as 'a good, moral political system', 'the best available political system', and 'acting in the national interest'. There may be various reasons for this, but one is surely that these would-be democratic features are rather *subjective and rhetorical* and difficult to *verify*; defining democracy in accordance with them may leave the door open to *any* political arrangement to be called democratic.

Third, note a key *tension* running through the definitions: the people ruling is a common thread here, but should the people *themselves* rule, or make decisions, or should their *representatives* do it? Between them, the definitions express a range of views on the issue. And fourth, note that a definition is only a definition; it is not a full theory, not the whole story; it does not account for all the institutions one might need to deliver on democracy's principles, and so on. In the next two chapters we will explore larger narratives that are built on specific definitions of democracy, and which tell fuller stories about what democracy ought to involve.

Dictionary and other definitions can help us to refine our earlier questions, derived from the case studies, but they also raise new ones. All these questions go to the heart of 'democracy'. The list of questions itself is not final, or definitive; democracy is always being re-created in new combinations and visions, a process made possible by the multiple and shifting significations that 'democracy' can and does provoke for various audiences. As I have suggested, dictionary and other definitions offer us *denotations* – what the word most immediately suggests. But they cannot easily silence the possibilities of *connotation*, a more elusive and plentiful set of potential meanings depending on audience(s), linguistic and cultural context, and so on. The elusiveness of precise meaning, and the shifting focus and range of the issues we would want to raise, are markers of the richness of meaning and the vital importance of democracy to our political lives (and even those who are 'not interested in politics' have political lives).

Having said that, it does seem that there are points of commonality, in the particular examples discussed and in the dictionary definition. Rule by the people or popular power is one claim which very commonly and plausibly accompanies evocations of 'democracy'. From the cases and the definitions we might conjecture that any suggested meaning that does not feature *evident popular power* may be suspect. And, linked with this, the ideas of equality and fairness seem to play a key role too. But it is never simply 'people power' or 'equality' or 'fairness' – in the abstract these things mean little, but in particular contexts they can have quite specific resonance, along with the power to engage and enervate people and consequently to revolutionize societies. Throughout later chapters we will have the opportunity to explore examples of past, present and (potential) future evocations of these ideals. I turn now from actual cases and arguments to a hypothetical puzzle. I do this to see if the challenge of having to design 'democratic' institutions forces us to resolve some of the questions that have arisen so far; or, at least, to see if it can show us more clearly the contours of the problems and dilemmas that seem to come with thinking in depth about democracy. So let us design a democratic system for an expectant country – country X.

How to design a democracy: country X

Country X is a distinctive place. Traditionally its population has been divided in terms of religion, language, politics and culture between three groups – the As making up 45 per cent, the Bs 35 per cent, and the Cs 20 per cent. They live and work together, by and large, but the three communities have a history of tension and mutual suspicion. How would you go about designing a democratic system for country X's national politics?

Immediately we confront what democracy *requires* of us and our institutions. I do not want to suggest there is one best way to respond to the challenge of country X (perhaps readers can think it through for themselves before moving on). But let us pursue one line of thought that will undoubtedly figure prominently whatever the precise approach adopted.

Consider the thought that one might worry from the start about *limiting* power in X as much as *allocating* it or making sure it is in the hands of 'all of the people'. For straight away we can see that a high level of agreement across the community in X on any significant political question is unlikely; will we need to embrace some form of majoritarian system, then, as a second-best solution? But how much should any electoral or other majority be able to impose a policy or obligation upon a minority that is unhappy with it (any two of the communities in X would be able to gang up on the third)? Could we act in some specific ways to protect minority 'rights' by limiting the powers of any given majority?

These thoughts might lead us in quite specific directions when considering which institutions a democratic X might adopt. First, in terms of voting or electoral systems, we would have a basic choice between a majoritarian system and a proportional system. Various specific electoral systems fit one of these categories more or less neatly – going into great detail here is not necessary. A majoritarian system would allocate seats in a parliament or legislature in a way that tends to create a legislative or governing majority out of an electoral minority. For example, as in the United Kingdom, a vote of less than 40 per cent of the electorate can generate a comfortable legislative majority. In country X, the use of such a system might grant group A a solid governing majority if its members vote as a bloc. Could we avoid this, democratically? A proportional system would (ideally at least) result in parties or blocs obtaining seats in the legislature in proportion to their votes; in X, this would be likely most often to result in no one community having a governing majority, which in turn would necessitate coalition or other cooperative forms of political behaviour (live and let live, agree to disagree, alternation in office, compromise, power-sharing).

But, second, what about the other institutions of government? Given concerns about potentially dangerous hostility between the three communities, we might want to ensure that agencies and departments in the national administration are not dominated by any one or two of the groups. Some form of proportionality might be something we would want to *extend* to administrative and other non-elective offices too. What about some form of separation of powers, a venerable tradition in democratic theory and practice and most famously incorporated in the constitution of the USA? A separation of powers might ensure (as far as institutional designs can guard against any particular outcomes) that no significant group in the society lacks the capacity to have its concerns heard. But perhaps, even more importantly, we might look at the nature and composition of the three communities more closely. Is each group geographically concentrated, or are the communities dispersed, living among one another? Either way, would adopting a *federal* system, in which lower levels of government and administration have a degree of autonomy from centrally determined policies, cement freedoms and rights across the whole community? If that were the conclusion, this would be a further restriction on majoritarianism.

Third, how would the basic political rule-book – the constitution – articulate the powers of the people and their governing institutions? A constitution limits or qualifies powers by creating them: what legislatures can decide, what rights people have, how those rights may themselves have limits (e.g., freedom of speech). What about the potentially difficult status of constitutional limitations themselves as *democratic* devices – generally presided over by judges who are not themselves elected, and therefore perhaps lacking democratic credibility? So far the groups have occupied our thinking centrally; perhaps individuals, their rights, their autonomy, deserve constitutional protection? Maybe, by emphasizing the rights of individuals, we take care of the rights of the groups, too?

And what about the *identities* of the groups and their members – should group cultures, religions or languages, for example, be recognized or protected officially (constitutionally) in country X? Maybe a group could feel it genuinely 'belonged' in the overall community if it felt that its culture was valued and protected by community law? Then again, would such a stipulation carry dangers of cementing into place just one, contestable version of what that group *is*, or what it represents? What if a group's culture encompassed, for example, systematic discrimination against girls and women?

In short (and too briefly): a democrat in cases such as this is quickly faced with some fundamental challenges and choices. Does 'democracy' demand majority rule or minority protection or both – and, if both, with what balance? Do groups or individuals matter most? Can and should electoral and other governing institutions at various levels be arranged so that no one group can dominate (all of) them at once – no matter who wins the elections?

I would like to make two observations about this outline reasoning. First, note some key assumptions that the above comments involve. I have assumed the importance of equal votes, and the need for some form of equality of (variously) power, protection and dignity between all citizens, regardless of religious or other cultural attachments and outlooks. I have also assumed that the primary form of political structure and activity, and the main means for the expression of popular power, will be representative, rather than (say) direct. Along with this, I assumed that a parliament or legislature was a necessary democratic body. There are other assumptions here which were not defended, but those are the main ones. Let me suggest that making these assumptions is (a) very common and (b) not so easy to defend as is commonly thought. Just how common they are, and how some influential writers on democracy have set out to defend them, we will see in some detail in the next chapter.

Going further, because a common tendency is to think about 'democratic designs' in terms of voting, parliaments, and so on, often we tend not to think of quite radically different – but not necessarily democratically 'wrong' – ways of organizing political affairs. Among the more radical or unconventional questions we could ask about country X are:

- Does one person, one vote, matter so much, when really it is fair representation of the different cultural communities that counts? Could we not institute instead a kind of quota system, where each community picks its own representatives?
- Why think that *votes* count that much? Voting is not necessarily or naturally *the* major mechanism for democracy. We are very used to regarding it as such – not a fact to be set aside lightly – but in logical terms it need not be. Why not *talk*, or better *deliberation*, instead, for example? Where collective decisions need to be reached, why not discuss the issues in groups until a form of consensus emerges – or, failing that, some workable form of 'agreement to disagree' at least?
- Why should community associations for each of the three groups not control its own affairs? Why do we have to think of them as needing to share joint governing institu-

tions – common 'parliament' and 'government', for example – rather than each controlling its own, quite separate, set of political institutions?

• Why not direct, or at least more participative, forms of democracy, rather than the concentration on forms of representation? Perhaps 'democracy' need not mean *maximizing* the people's power at every opportunity, but why would would-be democratic designers use as a kind of default mode an institutional arrangement – elections for representatives – that limits formal popular participation to marking ballot papers every so often?

Further, and perhaps most fundamentally: why is X 'a country'? What *made* it a country, that is, a single political unit? If those forces can be identified, how would we know if they were *democratic* forces? Would one or more of the groups prefer to constitute its *own*, separate and smaller country or political unit? As democrats, should we first look to organize a referendum to see if X should stay as *one* country at all? And, if so, who gets to vote – all members of all groups, or just the ones where there is pressure to secede?

One clear hypothetical example has led us to a sea of important and tricky questions. What can we learn from this brief effort to think about democratic design?

What does the problem of country X tell us? Issues for discussion

Looking at possibilities for country X as we have prompts the thought that there is no one, single, best way to have or to design a democracy. As with much else, when asked what a democracy should really look like, we have to say 'it all depends.' It depends on who makes up the political unit in question, what their goals and predilections are, and when we are talking about (designing a 'democracy' in 1820 or 1930 would be a radically different task from doing it in 2003, because different things were thinkable). It also depends on where the unit is (culture and geography have an impact on what the people will expect of 'democracy' and whether or not they will be prepared to embrace one or other version of it), why the issue of political change is on the agenda in the first place, and how it is proposed change might be achieved. Attempting to shape renewed democratic institutions in Lebanon after the civil war in the mid-1980s was a different task in these respects from the efforts in the Czech Republic in 1989 or South Africa in 1990.

Second, however, our case suggests that, although there is no one right answer, there are and have been various characteristic ways of thinking about the demands of democracy – different traditions, models or paradigms which suggest different sorts of responses. We are not adrift in a sea of wholly unconnected ideals and devices; various of these have conventionally been gathered together into more or less coherent visions of what democracy is, was, and can become. In particular, tangible evidence of popular power, along with political equality and a basic fairness, seem to have emerged as perhaps instinctively important to any would-be democracy on the basis of the cases and definitions examined in this chapter. Chapters 2 and 3 will chart a course through major late twentieth-century narratives of democracy to see how they construct approaches to democratic answers. From our cases and discussions in this chapter, we will see more clearly the range of questions these narratives will need to encompass and address.

Finally, the narratives considered in chapters 2 and 3 do not characteristically question the 'givenness', or the inevitability or naturalness, of the nation-state as *the* site for the practice of democracy. But the question of what might 'rightly' constitute a political unit which forms the appropriate subject for self-government haunts all approaches to the idea of democracy. Does 'democracy' ultimately depend on a given political unit which is unlikely itself to have come into being 'democratically' (rather than by war, conquest, violence generally)? In recent years the issue of the political unit has been asked more, and more trenchantly, than for some time. This change has been prompted by the fact of, and political concern about, 'globalization', the rise in number and intensity of sub-national demands for autonomy, and the increased political salience of culture and identity. In chapters 4 and 5 I will look, for example, at ecological

and other arguments that question in basic ways how boundaries (of various kinds) impact upon our thinking about the
possibilities of democracy.

Is democracy a good thing?

The issues prompted by our real and hypothetical examples
thus set the scene for more detailed discussions of the idea of
democracy as we move through the book. But now I want to
turn to the final main topic of this chapter. It is a topic that
has run through all that has been said so far, but we have not
pinpointed it in precise terms or drawn it out as yet. The issue
is – is democracy valuable? Is it the best form of political
system? If we value it, why is this the case, and *what* exactly
do we think we are valuing? Are there, should there be, limits
to the extent to which we think democracy is a good thing
(or a bad one, for that matter)?

The winner of the 1998 Nobel Prize for Economics,
Amartya Sen, looking recently over the history of democracy,
commented that:

> In any age and social climate, there are some sweeping beliefs
> that seem to command respect as a kind of general rule – like
> a 'default' setting in a computer program; they are considered
> right *unless* their claim is somehow precisely negated. While
> democracy is not yet universally practiced, nor indeed uni-
> formly accepted, in the general climate of world opinion,
> democratic governance has now achieved the status of being
> taken to be generally right. The ball is very much in the court
> of those who want to rubbish democracy to provide justifi-
> cation for that rejection. (Sen 1999, 5)

As Sen goes on to note, this status of democracy is a recent
phenomenon; it is only in the twentieth century, and largely
in the second half of that century, that the status was
achieved. The category of 'those who want to rubbish democracy' is a small one; few outright opponents proclaim themselves as such; and when we find them we might often regard
them as marginal, sometimes dangerous, extremists such as
racial or cultural or religious supremacists of one type or
another. Much more common, as we have seen in this chapter,

is the evocation of 'democracy' *in support of* goals which many would hesitate to associate with the idea of democracy at all. Such, again, is the power of the word, and in particular the power of its very ambiguity.

Meaning and justification, or, how democracy can be (constructed as) bad for you

Just as there are a range of arguments from political theorists and political philosophers as to *the* meaning of democracy, so there is a familiar set of arguments in this literature as to why democracy is a good thing. With their roots in the language of the discipline of philosophy, these debates are often referred to as being about 'the justification of democracy'. Political philosophy has given us some neat categories as to why democracy is indeed a (very) good thing, the best political thing. I will say more about what these are and what we might make of them in a moment. My main purpose in focusing on value here is to examine briefly the relationship between the 'justification' of democracy and the construction of its meaning. Like the task of definition, justification is about the *construction*, and not the *discovery*, of reasons and arguments. But first, let us again focus on examining a particular case to concentrate our thoughts: a recent argument from one of the world's leading historians suggesting in its title that 'democracy can be bad for you'.

Writing in March 2001, the eminent British historian Eric Hobsbawm cast doubts on the ability of democracy to respond effectively to new global, environmental and other challenges, and placed this in the context of searching questions that have long been asked of democracy's real value. I will look in chapter 4 specifically at these and other challenges, and in chapter 5 at proposed new forms of democracy that might help us to address some of them. Here, I concentrate on the questions that Hobsbawm raises about democracy's value, and what we can learn about debates over its value.

Asserting that the case for 'free voting' is that 'it enables the people (in theory) to get rid of unpopular governments', Hobsbawm raises three critical observations: first, liberal democracy requires a 'political unit' – and it 'is not applicable where no such unit exists'. Second, countries can be found where democratic government has not been accompanied by positive effects; in terms of economic prosperity or personal peace and security, for example, beneficial outcomes from democracy are not guaranteed. And third, he argues that 'the case for democracy is essentially negative', agreeing with Winston Churchill's comment that: 'Democracy is the worst form of government, except all those other forms that have been tried from time to time.' The technical nature of many current environmental and transport problems faced by democratic governments, for example, cannot be resolved by just asking the people, though some reasonable claim that policies represent the interests of the people must be present.

On one level, Hobsbawm's points act as reminders of earlier discussions. The first point reminds us that 'democracy' is normally thought of as belonging in a particular context – that of the 'country' or nation-state. One of the limits to its value is the restricted range of places and processes to which it might apply. Hobsbawm underlines this point by reminding us that 'Market sovereignty is not a complement to liberal democracy; it is an alternative to it.' In other words, democracy implies *government*, and the justifiability of government, in a defined political unit. The second point questions a longstanding argument in favour of democracy – that it produces beneficial outcomes, and therefore is a good thing (is 'justified'). What if it does not produce the benefits – or not unfailingly, in all contexts? The Churchill argument suggests that justifications which claim that democracy embodies certain basic principles we must all accept – political equality is a common candidate – overlook many flaws in democratic practice.

All of that is useful. But to jump to that level straight away – to consider the basic arguments for and against democracy – skips an important stage in thinking about democracy's value (mind you, we would be in good company if we did skip it). That is, it is never simply 'democracy', in itself, which is argued to be a good (or bad) thing; it is rather a *specific interpretation* of what democracy is. In order to praise or to criticize democracy, first one must construct its meaning – or borrow someone else's construction (such as one of the influential narratives considered in chapters 2 and 3).

Any attempt to offer a general or universally applicable justification for democracy must do something it would prefer not to do – namely, construct democracy's meaning in a particular way to make the argument intelligible in the first place. Hobsbawm, for example, does this early on in his article – democracy, for him, equates to 'the idea of competitively elected assemblies or presidents'. Elsewhere, he equates the deficiencies of democracy with the deficiencies of people voting. On the increasing range of complex technical issues governments have to deal with, 'democratic votes (or consumers' choices in the market) are no guide at all.' Solving global environmental problems 'will require measures for which, almost certainly, no support will be found by counting votes or measuring consumer preferences'. So, democracy is about people voting, and that is the problem because voting as a mechanism displays flaws which are at the same time the flaws of democracy itself.

But this is not the only way in which democracy can be understood or constructed, as we have seen. Though there are limits to what democracy can be taken to mean – it cannot be just anything that anyone has ever claimed it is – there remains wide scope for constructing it in different ways, and as a result *qualifying what might be said about its value* in a variety of ways too. Hobsbawm, for instance, does not consider that democracy could include mechanisms of discussion and deliberation along with that of voting; if it could, perhaps deliberative mechanisms might play a role in informing 'ignorant' popular opinion on pressing and complex issues. He also defines some innovative new possibilities out of the frame by stipulating that democracy can occur only within the confines of the nation-state. This particular stipulation rules out, for example, regarding new transnational networks in civil society (such as those opposed to so-called bio-piracy, or to the resumption of large-scale whaling) as forces which reshape and extend democracy's domain and potential (see discussion of the ideas of Held, Dryzek and others in chapters 4 and 5 below).

This is not to say that Hobsbawm is wrong – elected governments have been and remain a core part of what 'democracy' signifies – but rather that his assessment of the value of democracy is the product of a particular perspective; it might have been different if other, perhaps less traditional, perspectives on democracy were to be adopted.[7] In general terms, then, the question of democracy's value depends on the perspective adopted in order to assess it. It makes a big difference whether one starts with abstract theories and principles or specific cases; with one set of countries rather than another; with a broad and flexible definition of democracy or a narrower and more fixed one. Further, assessments of democracy's value depend on the interpretation of the challenges that democracy needs to overcome, for example, challenges of environmental degradation and economic globalization. Just how problematic and difficult such challenges are is itself contested, though; for instance, expert consensus on the threat of global warming is impressive.

Can it be right that there is no final, absolute justification for democracy? Is this not an uncomfortable position? It may be. But it may also be a liberating one. If there will always be some doubt over the real meaning and value of something, then this fact might act as a spur to the constant rethinking, and remaking, of that thing. A great many models and perspectives, from the past and present and for the future, will be canvassed in the following chapters; as we go through them, the benefits of fluidity and flexibility in helping us to confront new challenges should become clearer. Sometimes it is said that the answer to the problems of democracy is 'more democracy'; if so, we can expect that the 'more' will be not just more of the same, but something new which alters the character of the thing. Reflecting on Hobsbawm's argument, for example, democracy might need to stretch to encompass cross-border forms of mobilization outside the confines of the nation-state in response to the limited capacities of national democracy.

A strategic affection?

Finally, one crucial issue thrown up by this brief discussion of the value of democracy echoes one of the core concerns that arose from the discussion of definitions. Can we trust anyone to be disinterested, or more-or-less objective, on such issues? Is there anyone who offers an authoritative voice on democracy's value? Our discussion so far suggests that, although today just about everybody claims to love democracy, no one can love democracy *for its own sake*; all will love it only if so doing serves their strategic purposes.

On one level, this fact looks perfectly reasonable. Parties exist, interest groups exist, and politicians pursue careers to achieve certain outcomes (be these laudable political goals or more narrow self-advancement). Why have a disinterested love for a procedure – such as a democratic procedure – if it will not now, or may not in the future, help you to achieve the outcomes which are the things closest to your heart?

Even the democratic theorist has a strategic interest in democracy, in his or her preferred conception of it being widely accepted. Perhaps this is the secret of democracy's popularity; our love for democracy can be *reinforced* by the fact that there is scope to reconstruct the object of our affection in congenial ways. We can all continue to profess our love, safe in the knowledge that, quietly, we are loving different versions of the thing we refer to by a common name.

In the end, perhaps there is a certain necessary, and encompassing, hypocrisy when it comes to the value of democracy? The British political commentator Decca Aitkenhead put it well when she wrote: 'We are all implicated in the contradictions, for there is no such thing as a disinterested love of democracy in politics . . . Just as a belief in God didn't stop priests sinning, so democracy doesn't stop governments bending the rules – so long as they can get away with it.' This mutual implication, she suggests, is a fine (and acceptable) balance – 'what we require is that our politicians be sophisticated enough to pass off self-interest respectably. We are complicit in the pretence, but for us to collude they must make it credible . . . Democracy is not safeguarded by reference to some pure, abstract absolute. It is protected by the necessity of governments being able to get away with only so much' (Aitkenhead 1998). The academic commentators' lack of disinterest may be of a different order to that of the politician (though by no means always); it is no less real for that.

Conclusion

This chapter has used a variety of case materials to raise and to explore questions about democracy's meaning and value.

The main message has concerned the open-endedness of the term, about its lack of fixed or fixable meaning, within limits, and how this might impact upon our thinking about it. This open-endedness will prove a key point as we proceed.

Many of the points raised here are picked up and explored further in the following chapters.

Issues around the fertility of 'democracy' as a signifier were raised. The cases we looked at underlined the many ways in which actors use, or deploy, what they take to be democracy, in their efforts to win arguments or gain support; they also underlined the point that there is no easy way to maintain that 'democracy' is being used wrongly across these diverse contexts. Chapters 2 and 3 pick up on this theme, examining certain influential ways in which the term was reinterpreted and recast in its eventful recent history. Chapter 5, similarly, takes up the issue of how new significations of democracy try to respond to new challenges, such as that of globalization (see chapter 4).

We shall look at efforts to measure and to assess the quality of democracy in chapter 3, along with the issue of who if anyone can provide reliable criteria for democracy. Regarding the mix of institutions that 'democracy' requires – as in the hypothetical case of country X above – all remaining chapters will deal with a variety of views, mainstream and marginal. As part of this, the notion that democracy means many things rather than one thing will be addressed specifically as an issue for the interesting cases of 'Islamic democracy' and 'non-Western democracy' in chapter 4. Finally, the question of the political unit – which group of people is the right group to be subject to democracy – will be addressed in chapter 5 as we consider (e.g.) cosmopolitan and ecological conceptions of the extension of orthodox democratic practice beyond national boundaries, building on the discussion of globalization and related issues in chapter 4.

So, let us turn now to some influential constructions or narratives of democracy which have framed how many of us view democracy today.

2
Narrating Democracy I

> A way of seeing is always a way of not seeing.
>
> Kenneth Burke, *Permanence and Change*

Introduction

To offer a narration is to tell a story. In this case, it is a story which gives the idea of democracy a particular meaning and value. It is, at the same time, to dismiss or suppress alternative narratives which may subvert the preferred story. We saw in chapter 1, by exploring a variety of real-world and hypothetical examples, some of the main questions that come up once we start to interrogate the idea and practice of democracy. In this and the next chapters, we look at how different narratives have responded to some of these questions. But first a couple of introductory remarks about the idea of 'narrative', the historical context of these narratives, the focus on texts, and the idea of 'intertextuality'.

More often, these narratives are called 'theories' or 'models' of democracy, but I prefer to call attention to their story-like qualities by calling them 'narratives'. My main reasons for this are: (1) that a theory or model suggests a closed, finished, product, whereas the idea of narrative suggests – more accurately, in my view – that these ideas are more incomplete and open-ended than that; and (2) that a theory or model focuses our attention on what is *revealed* in the model-building process, where I feel it is often more productive to pinpoint what may be concealed. The proof of this approach will lie in the pudding, of course. It is consistent with the view taken in chapter 1, that 'democracy' is something that is constructed not discovered, and further that it is valuable because *we* value it, not because of some intrinsic or permanent property it possesses.

In this chapter, I focus on one broad and distinctive narrative of democracy, one which has been particularly influential in constructing twentieth-century Western orthodoxy about democracy. It is sometimes called the 'competitive elite' theory of democracy, sometimes the 'realist' theory. Getting a sense of its content, history and influence will take us directly on to examining critical counter-narratives – radical and alternative ways of understanding democracy such as Marxism and feminism – in chapter 3. It will also provide vital background to examining new challenges, and innovations for democracy which might help in the effort to meet those challenges, in chapters 4 and 5 respectively. I do not try to say everything that could be said about these key narratives, and others; what I offer is a broad sweep of connected ideas rather than close and detailed examination of any one of them.

In a similar vein, I offer little historical context or backdrop, concentrating instead on the *ideas*. History matters, of course, and ideas cannot simply be divorced from their contexts. However, for present purposes space permits only a tracing of key narratives themselves. It is worth bearing in mind, though, that a series of seismic changes in the way political life was seen and organized in the West in the nineteenth and especially the twentieth century run through all that will be covered in this chapter:

- the development of the modern state as a set of institutions – legislatures, courts and executives, for example – which rules the people in a fixed territory;
- the development of the modern sense of 'nation' to describe the people ruled by the state (e.g., the French people and the French state), and also partly the territory concerned (France inside its settled borders);

- the development of the idea of 'the people' as the main subject of political rule in the state, and as the legitimate source of political power (as opposed to the 'divine right of kings', for example);
- struggles between peoples and classes over the merits and demerits of democratizing political power, especially, for instance, regarding extensions of the right to vote (the franchise) from propertied men to all men, and later to women; and
- the impact of industrialization, urbanization and techno-logical advance upon production and war and state power.

These and related major historical developments are reflected, though not always in obvious ways, in the content and concern of the ideas discussed below. Ideas never arise and change in isolation from the world that produces them; as a scholar of ancient Greek democracy put it, 'The history of ideas is never just the history of ideas; it is also a history of institutions, of society itself' (Finley 1985, 11).

The ideas examined here will be explored in a particular way – through specific texts by contemporary and classical authors. These texts are well known and influential. This approach differs from the one I used in chapter 1, in that the authors of these texts aimed to integrate their ideas about democracy and to offer a coherent, single narrative – some-thing that (for example) the British Democracy Campaign was, understandably, too busy politicking to do. We might expect, then, that our narrative texts will begin to provide some answers – indeed, competing answers – to some of the fragmented questions thrown up by chapter 1.

Finally, to introduce one more piece of jargon, part of what we trace as we explore selected themes in these texts is 'intertextual' influences. These can operate in three ways:

- past texts influence the style and content of subsequent ones (the recent and the present filtered through the past);
- modern and contemporary texts shape how we read and interpret older texts (the past filtered through the present); and

- we as readers bring our own 'texts', our own understandings and prejudices and interpretive frames, to bear on particular texts and narratives that we read.

Part of what this chapter is about is tracing the *construction* of orthodoxy, of 'normal' and familiar (even seemingly natural) ways of seeing 'democracy' over approximately the past 200 years. We do well to remember in particular that we as readers are not passive in this process – constructions or narratives can only be 'natural' if we *allow* ourselves to receive them in that way.[1]

Reactions to pessimism: the views from the two World Wars

Democracy and the 'iron law of oligarchy'

Things did not look good for democracy in the midst of World War I. Writing in 1915, and contemplating 'This deplorable war, come like a storm in the night . . . with such a lack of respect for human life and of regard for the eternal creations of art as to endanger the very cornerstones of a civilization dating from more than a thousand years' (Michels [1915] 1968, 357), the German sociologist Robert Michels published what was to become one of the classics of political science. Called plainly *Political Parties*, the book charted 'the oligarchical tendencies of modern democracy'. It argued that, in modern, complex societies, all organizations – not least socialist parties which claimed to be strongly democratic in structure and outlook – have a tendency to oligarchy, that is, to become bureaucratic and to be run by an elite minority.

There were various reasons for this being the case, each compellingly argued in *Political Parties*. Above all, the demands on large-scale organizations (such as corporations, trade unions, universities, and so on) in the modern world are such that a relatively permanent, expert, professional leadership is unavoidable. This is the case even for organizations which profess radical democracy and equality for their internal affairs, and advocate the same for society at large.

There was, in Michels's words, an 'iron law of oligarchy': 'Democracy leads to oligarchy, and necessarily contains an oligarchical nucleus' (Michels [1915] 1968, 6). So even in a democracy, according to Michels, organizational elites will rule. Their domination becomes such that it is difficult to believe that democracy, in the sense of genuine equality of participation and influence in organizations and in society at large, is in fact possible at all. The main mechanism of elite domination is modern, large-scale organization, which cements into place an unclosable gap between the leaders and the led, elite and mass.

The Michelsian dilemma

Michels had to grapple with a crucial dilemma: that of the democrat whose observations convince him that democracy is not really attainable in practice. He was a friend of and an influence upon a founder of contemporary sociology, Max Weber, who himself famously struggled with the difficult political implications of the widespread and large-scale bureaucratization of social, political and economic organization, and he placed himself in a line with the other noted social theorists Gaetano Mosca and Vilfredo Pareto in what is now referred to as 'classical elite theory'. In the late nineteenth and early twentieth centuries, suspicion of the rise of 'democracy' through fear of uneducated, unruly and unrestrained popular power was common. Michels's own scholarly conclusions about the 'iron law' arising from his in-depth study of what was one of the first mass socialist parties, the German Social Democratic Party, led him to share, indeed to reinforce, the suspicion. But Michels was a socialist and a democrat, hence giving rise to what we can call the Michelsian dilemma: how to be a democrat when, objectively, democracy is not really possible. It contains a fatal flaw which eats it from the inside out, so to speak.

Michels wrote that 'Democracy is a treasure which no one will ever discover by deliberate search. But in continuing our search, in labouring indefatigably to discover the undiscoverable, we shall perform a work which will have fertile results in the democratic sense' ([1915] 1968, 368). *To discover the undiscoverable* – the tortured reasoning in this passage is evident enough. Ultimately, Michels resolved his dilemma for himself – but not necessarily for democrats more generally – by embracing Mussolini's Fascist regime in Italy in the 1920s. According to later writings, Michels now felt that the answer to the democratic dilemma lay in 'persons endowed with extraordinary congenital qualities, sometimes held to be justly supernatural and in every way always far superior to the general level. By virtue of these qualities such persons are deemed capable (and often they are) of accomplishing great things, and even miraculous things' (Michels 1949, cited in Lipset 1968).

Note, though, that the 'Michelsian dilemma' – the desperate search to discover the undiscoverable – arises only if democracy's meaning is constructed or understood in such a way as to provoke it into being. We saw in the previous chapter how important this is: what a given writer takes 'democracy' to signify will go a long way towards determining their attitude to its value and feasibility. For Michels, democracy signified something close to 'grassroots democracy', a strongly levelling and egalitarian conception of how participation within a large-scale organization, and in society at large, should work. Almost any kind of established leadership structure would seem to undercut what Michels *regarded as* 'democracy'.

So Michels's conclusions about democracy's tendencies, and his own ultimate abandonment of democracy, were not so unusual in the aftermath of World War I. The 1920s and 1930s were a time when the advancing tide of democracy appeared first to slow down and then to recede, with the establishment of varied forms of dictatorship and totalitarianism of the left and the right in Russia, Germany, Italy, Japan and other countries. But Michels's conclusion was not the only one that could be reached, even if his arguments about the 'iron law of oligarchy' are largely accepted. It all depends what you think is 'oligarchy', and what 'democracy'. Consider the comment of Seymour Martin Lipset, writing in his Introduction to an edition of Michels's *Political Parties*:

> Democracy in the sense of a system of decision-making in which all members or citizens play an active role in the

continuous process is inherently impossible. Organization elites in general do not have long-term tenure in office. Michels clearly demonstrated the technical impossibility of terminating the structural division between rulers and ruled within a complex society. Political and organizational elites have special group interests which are somewhat at variance with those of the people they represent. But even if we accept all of these points as valid, they do not mean that democracy is impossible; rather *they suggest the need for a more realistic understanding of the democratic potential in a complex society*. (Lipset 1968, 34–5, italics added)

The realist narrative: Schumpeterianism

Writing in the United States during World War II, against the background of the rise of Fascism in Western Europe apparently through mobilizing mass popular support, the economist Joseph Schumpeter, a former finance minister in Austria, provided just such a 'more realistic understanding'. Schumpeter's answer to the Michelsian dilemma was to prove highly influential, and that influence can be seen clearly in dominant ways of thinking about democracy today, almost sixty years after the publication of his classic book *Capitalism, Socialism and Democracy*. Critics of mainstream views of democracy target Schumpeter's view above all (as we shall see in the following chapter). For these and other reasons his account provides a useful pivot in our exploration of democracy's key narratives.

Schumpeter argued that 'classical', pre-twentieth century, theories of democracy were unrealistic and outdated. They could provide little by way of a theory of democracy suitable for the complex, bureaucratic, mass societies of the twentieth century. What was needed was 'another theory of democracy which is much truer to life and at the same time salvages much of what sponsors of the democratic method really mean by this term' (Schumpeter [1943] 1976, 269). Schumpeter's much-quoted preferred definition of democracy is as follows: 'the democratic method is that institutional arrangement for arriving at political decisions in which individuals acquire the power to decide by means of a competitive struggle for the people's vote' ([1943] 1976, 269).

(Readers might compare this definition with those discussed in the previous chapter.)

This definition sounds familiar notes to the contemporary ear. It speaks of 'individuals' to a set of Western and other societies much more individualistic over half a century after he wrote, and of competitive voting when this device is seen as being critical to democracy. It seems 'realistic' in that, apparently, it describes the essence of political reality in our modern mass societies – that elected representatives rule. But familiarity can blind us to the assumptions and character of arguments, and to the fact that they are not natural but constructed. We need to dig deeper into Schumpeter's influential formulation, looking briefly at democracy as a method, competitive elite politics, leadership, and the role of ordinary people.

Democracy as a method Note, first, that for Schumpeter democracy is just a *method*. It is not about ideals, or ends, such as the achievement of justice or the betterment of peoples. All that need concern us, it is saying, are procedures by which decisions are reached, *means* and not *ends*. Throughout its long history the idea of democracy has been linked to a variety of ends – a more egalitarian society, the general interest, the maximization of freedom, and so on. In these approaches, the value of democracy is said to reside in the fact that it produces these important benefits. But Schumpeter wants to detach democracy from such high-flown goals and claims. There are no guarantees, he says, that a democratic system will produce any particular sort of outcome, or result in the practical realization of any particular ideal. Democracies may in fact produce socially desirable outcomes, but they do not *start* with that in mind – rather, 'we must start from the competitive struggle for power and office and realise that the social function is fulfilled, as it were, incidentally – in the same sense as production is incidental to the making of profits' ([1943] 1976, 282).

Competitive elite politics Second, the economist's definition invites us to see politics through the lens of the competitive economic market. The concept of competition for leadership, Schumpeter writes, 'presents similar difficulties as the concept of competition in the economic sphere, with which it may be usefully compared' ([1943] 1976, 271).

Schumpeter's political sphere revolves around a rather exclusive, high-level battle between elite actors; it is about individuals who achieve legitimate advantage or positions of leadership by virtue of successful competitive struggle in elections. Politicians are entrepreneurs, attempting to sell packages of policies to voters ('consumers'). The market metaphor is pervasive. The marketplace is the zone of self-interest, competition, winners and losers, and of 'what sells' and sometimes 'what works'; it is not, for better or for worse (I do not write in judgement), a zone of shared goals, collective endeavour or conscious and organized pursuit of the general interest.

Proposing leaders, not imposing   Third, the basic distinction that Schumpeter's definition offers between democracy and totalitarianism is not equality versus inequality, the people ruling versus the people being ruled, or any other piece of misty-eyed romanticism. Rather, it is simply that in a democracy leaders *propose* themselves, while in a totalitarian state leaders *impose* themselves. Democracy is all about the exercise of leadership and who gets legitimately to exercise it; Schumpeter's approach, he tells us, 'leaves all the room we may wish for a proper recognition of the vital fact of leadership' ([1943] 1976, 270). Michels's fear has become Schumpeter's mainstay.

It is important to note in this context that, although Schumpeter offers us many reasons for defining democracy in the way that he does, some of them arise not from his 'realism' but from the kinds of methods of analysis he thinks that political scientists ought to deploy. One important advantage, as he sees it, of his preferred definition is that it provides 'a reasonably efficient criterion by which to distinguish democratic governments from others'; it stresses the importance of a procedure, 'the presence or absence of which it is in most cases easy to verify' ([1943] 1976, 269, 270). That seems an admirable, scholarly goal. But to what extent is Schumpeter's definition driven by *measurability*, by the need to make the term *operationalizable*, that is, rendering it amenable to statistical and other forms of observational political science research? And if it was thus driven, does it matter? I return to this question below (and in chapter 4).

Can the people be trusted? Fourth, and crucially, ordinary people have very little role to play in Schumpeter's version of democracy. In the definition, all they get to do is 'vote' – it is clear that the 'individuals' to which the definition refers are elected leaders only. So 'the people' do not *decide policies*; political participation for the vast majority of people in a Schumpeterian democracy consists of voting occasionally for candidates in competitive elections. This point reinforces the fact that the theory focuses firmly on leadership.

The main reason for Schumpeter downgrading the role of ordinary people in democratic politics is straightforward enough: it is because most people are ignorant about the issues, irrational in their opinions and preferences, and easily swayed by manipulative appeals from unscrupulous politicians. Following on from Michels, who had no doubts about the general 'incompetence of the masses' when it came to political questions, Schumpeter thought that research had demonstrated conclusively the irrational tendencies of most people. He wrote that 'the typical citizen drops down to a lower level of mental performance as soon as he enters the political field. He argues and analyses in a way which he would readily recognize as infantile within the sphere of his real interests. He becomes a primitive again' ([1943] 1976, 262). The citizens' role is perfectly clear, in *this* democracy; they should vote, and 'understand that, once they have elected an individual, political action is his business and not theirs' ([1943] 1976, 295). The role of the electors is to produce a government, no more and no less. Schumpeter has a good deal to say about the qualities of leaders, and the need for restraint and expertise in government (he was fond of features of the English system of government as he saw it, since apparently it delivered on many of these desired qualities). But in all he says, the people have remarkably little role to play in this democracy.

The absent gender Note, finally, who these leaders were to be – men, pretty much exclusively. Schumpeter writes, for example, of 'the quality of the men the democratic method selects for positions of leadership'. Women get a different sort of mention; in the context of arguing that people's will is often manipulated and 'manufactured', 'The picture of the prettiest girl that ever lived will in the long run prove powerless to maintain the sales of a bad cigarette' ([1943] 1976, 263). But this is irrelevant, isn't it? 'Men' meant 'men and women', and the latter quote is just a throwaway line? Maybe. But feminist critics might disagree, as we shall see when we look at certain counter-narratives in the next chapter.

Finding democracy in oligarchy

I have dwelt on Schumpeter's theory because it is pivotal in certain key respects. Above all, it was his theory that set the tone for mainstream understandings of democracy in the post-war period. It took the Michelsian dilemma and turned it on its head, making elite rule the very essence of democracy, not its deadly nemesis. As Giovanni Sartori has written, in agreement with Schumpeter, 'democracy' can start where Michels stops: 'no matter how oligarchic the organization of each minority turns out to be when examined from within, even then the result of the competition between them is, in the aggregate, democracy' (Sartori 1987, 1.151). This view, this way of constructing democracy or attaching it to key signifieds such as 'leadership' and 'competition', remains highly influential, as we shall see next as we move on to extensions of the Schumpeterian narrative in post-war writing. One can imagine how it served the interests of elected leaders to buy versions of this narrative; they could enjoy, in principle, a legitimate concentration of power in their own hands and at the same time defend it as 'democracy'.

Variations on a theme: post-Schumpeterian thinking in Downs, Dahl and Lijphart

After World War II, and after the winning alliance had descended into the mutual suspicion and vilification, arms building, proxy confrontation and ideological posturing of the Cold War, the Schumpeterian democratic narrative found receptive audiences among those most concerned to describe and explain the fundamental character of democracy. I trace here threads in particularly influential post-war texts by Anthony Downs, Robert A. Dahl and Arend Lijphart. I do not suggest that these authors – each of whom has brought a distinctive voice to thinking about democracy – can or should be shoehorned into one, Schumpeterian, template. I have chosen to examine texts by these authors in the context of Schumpeterianism because, at one key level, they give new life to that narrative by adapting and refining it. I would not deny that there are other reasonable interpretations of these authors' texts, or that their writings beyond these texts might offer alternative views. As ever in this book, my focus is a close one and I do not pretend to cover everything. Looking at texts by these writers, albeit briefly, will enable us to trace the path of the dominant Schumpeterian narrative about democracy up to the end of the twentieth century.

Democratic politics as a marketplace: Downs

Anthony Downs's *An Economic Theory of Democracy*, first published in the USA in 1956, took certain themes from Schumpeter and moulded them into a blend with new ideas to produce a set of arguments about democracy that retains its influence nearly half a century later. There is little doubt about the Schumpeterian link; Downs writes that 'Schumpeter's profound analysis of democracy forms the inspiration and the foundation for our whole thesis, and our debt and gratitude to him are great indeed' (Downs 1956, 29).

An 'economic' theory? The key point about Downs's *An Economic Theory of Democracy* is the way he chooses to see democracy, the lenses he puts on to analyse it (and clearly he sees himself *analysing*, not criticizing or applauding). It is critical to understand how the gaze he adopts moulds and shapes in its turn the very subject of the gaze – 'democracy'. In a number of ways, this key point picks up Schumpeterian traces. The gaze that Downs adopts is clear from his book's title – this is an *economic* theory of democracy. This could mean various things – we might imagine it means how private companies or firms are governed in their internal affairs, for example. But for Downs it means that he wants us to look at democracy through the eyes, through the assumptions, of the economist.

Economists, most of the time, assume that men and women are *rational actors*, in the sense that they will choose the least costly means to achieve whatever ends or goals they happen to have. (Note that economists do not say that all people really *are* rational in this sense, merely that if we *assume* they are it helps us to clarify and analyse social life.) Downs makes this assumption about political actors: voters and politicians. The rational voter, for example, will vote for a politician or a party which promises to deliver most of what he or she wants. Likewise, the rational political party will try to maximize its vote in order to stay in office, or to gain office (in other words, to remain or to become the government). Democratic politics is about the competition for power that ensues between rational actors in these senses.

We have seen how Schumpeter viewed politics as a competitive struggle analogous to the competition of the economic marketplace. Downs took this insight and made it much more formal and even more central to our understanding of democracy. In this way, Downs's analysis reinforces a distinctive set of choices, put into play by Schumpeter, about how 'democracy' should be viewed, making those choices mainstream, normal, somehow seemingly 'natural'.

Describing, analysing and recommending   Viewing politicians and voters as rational, self-interested, competitive actors has knock-on effects for how the accompanying vision of democracy is produced or constructed. In particular, note that the methodology drives the lack of concern for moral ends, or for the purposes of government, democracy or participation, at the heart of the Downsian understanding of democracy. Thus, on the one hand, 'politicians in our model never seek office as a means of carrying out particular policies; their only goal is to reap the rewards of holding office *per se*. They treat policies purely as means to the attainment of their private ends, which they can reach only by being elected' (Downs 1956, 28); and 'each citizen casts his vote for the party he believes will provide him with more benefits than any other' (1956, 36). This is fair enough – Downs is trying to hone tools to explain politics, not to moralize about it, or to change it. He writes that 'we try to describe what *will* happen under certain conditions, not what *should* happen' (1956, 20). And further, 'To avoid ethical premises, we define democratic government descriptively, i.e., by enumerating certain characteristics which in practice distinguish this form of government from others' (1956, 20). These 'certain characteristics' are thoroughly Schumpeterian: parties competing for the right to wield government powers for a limited period in free and fair elections (I paraphrase – see Downs 1956, 23).

Let's pause for a moment here, because some interesting things are happening. Note that Downs is describing what he thinks 'democracy' is, for the purposes of analysis, but insists that there is nothing 'ethical' going on, that his account is factual or descriptive. On one level, the distinction, and the way in which Downs pursues it, seems more than reasonable; there *is* a difference between describing and prescribing, or between explaining and recommending. Yet the model he describes and seeks to explain – a familiar one built around elections, competition, self-interest and representation – is a quite particular one, certainly not the only one he *could* have described. If Downs's model is an abstract version of a system like that of his native USA in the 1950s, and he is offering that as an accurate representation of 'democracy' generally, is that reasonable? Recall too that Schumpeter liked his 'realistic' view of democracy because observers who applied it to the political world would at least have a clear basis on which to judge which countries were democracies and which were not. Downs appears to take this point a stage further; it is largely about the *analysis*, about the measurability, about setting up hypotheses and being able to test them by gathering data (e.g., about election turnout or numbers of votes for parties). It is, in short, about political *science*, about studying politics in a scientific, objective manner.[2] In Downs's eyes, the job of political scientists such as him was to describe and analyse *how* democracy worked in practice, not waste time arguing about values or about how it *ought* to work.

The context of 'political science' The home of strong movements for an explanatory, as opposed to normative, political science was the USA in the period Downs was writing. At this time, the USA was locked in ideological as well as strategic-military struggle with the Soviet Union. Everyone knew, and only a small fringe minority in the USA questioned, that America was democratic and pluralist, while Soviet communism was anti-democratic, totalitarian in ideology and monolithic in organization. If you wanted to analyse 'democracy', and the USA was the exemplar of democracy, then what you needed to analyse was a system like that of the USA – a neat circle (Holden, 1974, calls this the 'definitional fallacy'). But of course the USA at that time represents only one vision of what democracy might mean, or look like – however difficult it may have been to see this point at that time. This is a general problem in political analysis. Scientific neutrality is a laudable aim. But our models and definitions do have a context, an origin, which is not itself 'neutral' or equally applicable to all. It is not an argument against Downs's *An Economic Theory of Democracy*, or a dismissal of its rigour, to point this out. It is merely to say that, however carefully one might separate explanation from recommendation, something of the latter inevitably threatens to undermine the integrity of the former. We will pursue this point further when we listen to critics of Schumpeterian approaches in the following chapter.

Downs's methods and assumptions echo and serve to reinforce many of Schumpeter's: the individualism, the idea of competition for office, the idea that representation is central to democracy, and the fact that we must study democracy with a keen concern for measurability *built into* our very methods and models. Each of these echoes or traces is a product of, or sits comfortably alongside, the aspiration to offer a value-free, descriptive account of democracy. This, incidentally, leads to some curious statements, and I mention one here in part because it raises issues about women and sexual equality which critics pick up. When he outlines the characteristics of a democratic system as he defines it, Downs writes (in a throwaway line) that, 'In some democracies, women or permanent resident aliens or both are not allowed to vote' (1956, 23). I point out simply that (a) a comment such as this is rendered perfectly natural due to the definition of democracy Downs uses, and (b) on other, reasonable, grounds it is an odd, highly questionable, statement. Again, a seemingly neutral definition in which nothing 'ethical' is intended turns out to contain assumptions which are nothing if not contestable in ethical terms.

No more agonizing More generally, note that Downs's work is entirely devoid of Michelsian agonizing; Schumpeter has, so to speak, 'won' that argument. 'Democracy' can, indeed does, mean competitive elections, fundamentally – all else, all higher or more egalitarian aspirations, involve little more than delusional posturing. Because Schumpeter has won that argument, Downs no longer needs to spell out the original problem. In a sense, Downs can be straightforwardly 'analytical' because the *ideological* work has been done by his predecessor. The people not participating beyond occasional votes, for example, is just not an issue for Downs – for that *is* democracy, and the interesting thing is to deduce hypotheses about how parties will compete for votes given the self-interest axiom that Downs begins with. And indeed, the focus and culmination of Downs's theory is a set of twenty-five 'testable propositions derived from the theory' (1956, 295–300).

The world of polyarchy: Dahl

I pause over Downs's theory because it sets out in rather severe and sparse terms assumptions about what democracy was, and could be, in the dominant narrative of the post-war West (namely, US, and US-influenced, political science and its varied audiences). In some ways the vision of democracy concerned could be a radical, critical tool for existing systems, including that of the USA – think of the critical value of a theory of the importance of *fair* elections in a democracy in the context of Florida 2000 (see chapter 1). But more often it stood as the exemplar of what democracy really meant and represented in the real world, a bulwark against overly radical and idealistic visions of politics and democracy. It is useful to discuss at this point key aspects of the work of probably the greatest post-war theorist of democracy, Robert A. Dahl. Specifically, I want to mention his idea of 'polyarchy', because it both captures and extends the broadly post-Schumpeterian view of democracy and its limits that has been sketched to this point. Dahl is also interesting because he both absorbs and extends the dominant Schumpeterian narrative, on the one hand, and in more normative mode is one of the most trenchant critics of the limits of American democracy, on the other.

The elements of polyarchy   Beginning with the publication of *A Preface to Democratic Theory* in 1956, Dahl (among other things) expounded the usefulness of the idea of 'polyarchy'. This concept has been taken by Dahl and others to refer to a range of things over the years, but in essence it means standards of democracy suitable for the 'real world', a kind of minimal level of democracy that can be expected or demanded of countries that claim to be democracies. Although quite a demanding standard, its features are ones familiar from Schumpeter and subsequent Schumpeterian thinking about democracy. Being a realist, Dahl was concerned in his early work not to expect too much of real countries, not to place the bar of 'democracy' so high that few or no countries could jump it. In his 1989 classic *Democracy and its Critics*, Dahl elucidated various threads of the idea of polyarchy:

> Polyarchy can be understood in several ways: as a historical outcome of efforts to democratize and liberalize the political institutions of nation states; as a distinctive type of political order or regime different in important ways not only from nondemocratic systems of all kinds but also from earlier small-scale democracies; as a system (*a la* Schumpeter) of political control in which the highest officials in the government of the state are induced to modify their conduct so as to win elections in political competition with other candidates, parties, and groups; as a system of political rights; or as a set of institutions necessary to the democratic process on a large scale. (Dahl 1989, 218–19)

Though each of these senses differs, I suggest that the idea of polyarchy as a specified minimal level of democracy, attuned to the realistic possibilities of the extent of democratization that is feasible, captures each of them.

But what institutions, what features, make up this minimally acceptable democracy? The following list, familiar to political scientists all over the world, expresses many things. One important feature within our present discussion is how it both fits with the basic thrust of Schumpeterian approaches to democracy, and extends and deepens post-Schumpeterianism in key ways. The institutions of polyarchy, as expressed in *Democracy and its Critics* (p. 221), are:

1   Elected officials. Control over government decisions about policy is constitutionally vested in elected officials.
2   Free and fair elections. Elected officials are chosen in frequent and fairly conducted elections in which coercion is comparatively uncommon.
3   Inclusive suffrage. Practically all adults have the right to vote in the election of officials.
4   Right to run for office. Practically all adults have the right to run for elective offices in the government, though age limits may be higher for holding office than for the suffrage.
5   Freedom of expression. Citizens have a right to express themselves without the danger of severe punishment on political matters broadly defined, including criticism of officials, the government, the regime, the socio-economic order, and the prevailing ideology.
6   Alternative information. Citizens have a right to seek out alternative sources of information. Moreover, alternative sources of information exist and are protected by laws.
7   Associational autonomy. To achieve their various rights, including those listed above, citizens also have a right to form relatively independent associations or organizations, including independent political parties and interest groups.

This list from 1989 looks quite different from the first one Dahl produced in 1956. The earlier one stressed *elections and voting* more narrowly and in more formal depth. It divided the conditions of polyarchy into (e.g.) characteristics 'during the voting period' and those 'during the interelection stage' (1956, 84). This emphasis provides the clearest clue as to what Dahl's approach added to that of Schumpeter: a concern for what happens *between* elections, which is most of the time, of course. The later, revised, set of characteristics and institutions of polyarchy cited above deepens this addition, by specifying rights to freedoms of expression and organization and information-gathering that are part of the routine of what is normally thought of as being 'democratic' politics. These rights and freedoms are, of course, crucial to the conduct of elections, but their importance extends beyond that immediate period or context. When we read Schumpeter, we get the sense that, once elections have been conducted and leaders have been chosen, it is entirely up to those leaders what they do. Dahl's polyarchy moves the dominant approach to post-war thinking about democracy away from that narrow interpretation.

Describing and measuring   That said, polyarchy is intended to be 'realistic', operationalizable, 'measurable'; it emphasizes (free and fair) competition for power as being at the heart of democratic politics; and it is the product of concern that classical ideals of democracy get in the way of proper, empirical appraisals of democracy and its possibilities. These features, each of which underlines the roots of the idea of polyarchy in what we have called Schumpeterian thinking, are particularly evident in the work of the early Dahl. In *A Preface to Democratic Theory*, Dahl makes it clear that, even if one starts with 'ethical' or value-based criteria of democracy, one soon needs to employ an approach that is truer to the 'real world'. Such an approach he calls 'the descriptive method': this involves considering 'as a single class of phenomena all those nation states and social organizations that are commonly called democratic by political scientists, and by examining the members of this class to cover, first, the distinguishing characteristics they have in common, and, second, the necessary and sufficient conditions for social organizations possessing these characteristics' (1956, 63). This approach is the root of polyarchy: *description* lies at its heart. This being the case aids a further goal – that in principle the characteristics of polyarchy would be *measurable* (though Dahl does not think this will be a straightforward matter). Crucially, of course, in-principle measurability drives, to a discernible extent, the presentation of polyarchy as a superior way of defining and understanding 'democracy'.

Dahl's early texts are more often criticized than read. *A Preface to Democratic Theory* is a complex and subtle text which by no means sets aside democratic norms or ideals, and is not uncritical towards the USA or other existing 'democracies'. In addition, from his earliest work Dahl has shown a strong interest in local democracy and workplace democracy which has influenced thinking in the participatory democracy tradition (see his later 'preface' – *A Preface to Economic Democracy* (1985) – and the discussion in chapter 3). Nevertheless the *Preface to Democratic Theory*, more than any other text by Dahl, shows the Schumpeterian roots of the idea of polyarchy. Further, the *Preface* does go some way to celebrate the American system of democracy, as a key exemplar of polyarchy (1956, 74), and in extended passages which celebrate the pluralistic politics of the USA in which 'The making of government decisions ... is the steady appeasement of relatively small groups' (1956, 146); in the 'normal' American political process, 'there is a high probability that an active and legitimate group in the population can make itself heard effectively at some crucial stage in the process of decision' (1956, 145).

Majority and consensus: Lijphart

Description, competitive elections, measurability and realism, a liking for US democracy and a suspicion of 'ethical' approaches: these themes are becoming familiar in our tracing of this narrative of democracy, even if (for example) Dahl is clearly a more radical and critical democratic theorist than Schumpeter. Of course I am being selective in the authors and texts I mention and which features I highlight; but these are the texts, writers and themes which largely defined the dominant Western post-war narrative. I turn now to a fourth influential exponent of this particular narrative line, Arend Lijphart.

I pick up on the work of Lijphart as exemplified in his two major works, *Democracies* (1984) and *Patterns of Democracy* (1999), since he takes a step further the institutional, 'realistic', measurable, competitive strand of theorizing about democracy that we have traced from Schumpeter's response to the Michelsian dilemma. (We shall see in the next chapter how, by the time Lijphart's major works were published, a number of other democratic narratives, muted in the heyday of post-Schumpeterianism in the 1950s and 1960s, were competing strongly with this one.)

Two models of democracy   Lijphart's key contribution to the narrative was to describe two models of democracy which between them account for most major political systems across the world that could conventionally be called democratic. In a sense, he splits the category of polyarchy into two, setting out *majoritarian* and *consensus* models. Certainly in Schumpeter and the early Dahl and Downs, democracy is conceived in majoritarian terms (although, more correctly, 'pluralitarian' – see discussion below): each citizen's vote counts for one, and no more than one, and the greater number of votes determines who wins elections. But Lijphart, in his observations (in *Patterns of Democracy*) of thirty-six countries around the world, concludes that most democracies are 'consensus' rather than 'majoritarian' democracies. This matters because (contrary to conventional wisdom as he sees it) 'consensus democracy may be considered more democratic than majoritarian democracy in most respects' (Lijphart 1999, 7). We can see here that, within his explanatory framework, Lijphart was ready to make explicit normative points.

Our main interest in Lijphart, in tracing our narrative, lies as much in *how* he does things as what he does – and in turn how his methods and assumptions shape his distinctive perspective on democracy. Let's outline the two models to fix our thoughts.

Majoritarian democracy   The majoritarian model, exemplified above all by the United Kingdom, displays the following institutional characteristics:

• executive power concentrated in one party, which forms the government on its own;

- the cabinet, consisting of government ministers, dominating the parliament;
- electoral dominance by two parties; though minor parties may win some seats in parliamentary elections, they can never win enough to form the government;
- an electoral system (the rules by which elections are conducted and votes counted) that favours majoritarian outcomes, exaggerating the support of bigger parties to produce parliamentary majorities for the winning party, even if that party did not gain a majority of the popular vote;
- interest groups tending to operate in a system of 'free-for-all pluralism', a kind of dynamic free market of ideas outside the government but attempting to influence it;
- unitary and centralized government, in that all subordinate political units and jurisdictions (such as elected local government) owe their existence and powers to the grace of the central government;
- concentration of legislative power in just one legislative chamber;
- constitutional flexibility, in that there is no written constitution which is difficult to change;
- absence of judicial review, in that (again) there is no 'higher' law to appeal to above legislative political outcomes;
- a central bank controlled by the executive.

Consensus democracy   In the 'pure' type of majoritarian model, power is concentrated and relatively unconstrained rather than dispersed and limited. The 'pure' consensus model provides a direct contrast. It has the following institutional characteristics (Lijphart 1999, 34–41):

- executive power-sharing in broad coalition cabinets;
- a balance of power between executive and legislature;
- a multiparty system (that is, more than two 'major' parties);
- proportional electoral systems, in which the number of seats a party wins in the legislature reflects reasonably closely the percentage of votes it received in an election;

- interest group corporatism, in which certain interest groups such as trade union and business 'peak' organizations work with, and within, the government on a regular basis;
- federal and decentralized government;
- strong bicameralism, or more-or-less equal powers shared between two legislative chambers;
- constitutional rigidity;
- judicial review;
- central bank independence.

Belgium and Switzerland exemplify many aspects of the consensus model in Lijphart's argument.

With this analysis, in many ways Lijphart takes us some way *beyond* Schumpeterianism – as was the case with the selected work of Dahl I examined above. To trace one key narrative line between texts is not to deny the significance of differences between them. However, I would argue that in key respects Lijphart reinforces and extends post-Schumpeterian assumptions about how we should look at democracy, bringing those assumptions up to the present day in the process. In this, he joins others in reinforcing the post-Schumpeterian narrative's grip on mainstream conceptions of democracy, precisely by changing it so it might adapt to new empirical circumstances and theoretical developments.

First, it is measurability, or operationalizability, which is the driving force behind Lijphart's work, as it was key to Schumpeter, Downs and Dahl in their different ways. These are all *empirical* models of democracy, concerned with 'real-world' institutional descriptions and explanations, and only really comfortable calling 'democracy' those national political systems that commonly are called democracies. Lijphart's particular focus is on quantitative data about (e.g.) numbers of parties in government coalitions, and electoral outcomes, in his various subject countries. His main goal is to provide empirical generalizations about different versions of democracy, and values do come into the picture for him because he clearly advocates adoption of consensus rather than majoritarian models to newly democratizing countries. These value judgements, however, build directly from and can make little sense without the limited, focused, empirical inquiry which precedes them.

Can the cases fit the mould? Note, though, that Lijphart has to go to some lengths at various points to retain the simplicity of his schema. He admits that the UK, the key example of the majoritarian model, is not really majoritarian but 'pluralitarian', since the legislative majorities are 'manu-factured' due to the nature of the electoral system (1999, 15). It becomes clear, too, that his consensus democracies are still majoritarian; it is just that governments in these systems normally consist of parties which add up to more than a bare majority (51 per cent) of the electorate in terms of the national vote. Further, in the more recent book he wishes to include the European Union as one of his thirty-six 'countries' – a brave and interesting decision, since the EU is not a 'country' or a 'nation', but a loose union of several nations each of which retains considerable, independent national powers. In particular, the EU's institutional structure is not characteristic of either of Lijphart's models of national democracy; Lijphart has to call the European Commission, an executive body consisting of unelected national nominees, his 'cabinet', and even the Council of Ministers of the EU, consisting of ministers of the different member countries, the 'upper house' of his bicameral legisla-ture (!) (1999, 42ff). In short, awkward cases that do not really fit his categories must be renamed and squeezed into those categories – in the name of measurability, comparabil-ity and empirical generalization.

It is not only in its methodological approach and concerns that Lijphart's work echoes and expands upon other post-Schumpeterian patterns. Its focus is relentlessly national (rather than local, and, given how he treats the EU, rather than supra-national as well); representative and indirect; and centred on questions of institutional structures at the centre of government, and consequently on questions of power and leadership. With respect to the representative or indirect focus, it is interesting that in *Democracies* Lijphart had a sep-arate chapter on referendums or direct democracy; this had disappeared in *Patterns of Democracy*. So, this is a detailed, wide-ranging, sophisticated analysis of important features of political systems we commonly call democratic. It is, at the same time, an analysis which picks up and adapts influential received ways – post-Schumpeterian ways – of seeing democracy, and of constructing its meaning and characteristics.

Summary: the core of the Schumpeterian narrative of democracy

Much more could be said on this particular narrative of democracy, but let us draw some threads together at this point to conclude the chapter. We might summarize the Schumpeterian approach by saying that it has been:

1   concerned to offer models that are 'realistic', measurable, and fitted with common assumptions about what 'democracy' means;
2   national in focus, to the extent that it is concerned with the institutional structure of central government above all;
3   indirect or representative in focus, seeing democracy as being about leadership and methods of selecting leaders, rather than about popular participation in politics as such;
4   individualistic in orientation, focusing on the individual as the main unit of political life, and working largely from liberal assumptions that individuals are self-interested in their political and other activities and goals;
5   concerned with democracy primarily as a method or a means, and not as a goal or an end; as something to be defined and analysed here and now, not set up as a more radical and probably unrealistic future aspiration;
6   egalitarian, but only in a formal sense of highlighting equal votes and equal political rights; and less concerned, in this respect, with economic or social equality; and
7   concerned to describe what is, rather than prescribe what ought to be.

These summary points overlap with each other in various ways. Not each of them is equally applicable to the texts of each of the authors discussed briefly in this chapter. Dahl in particular has a radical and normative edge in *some* of his work which challenges (e.g.) the limits of formal equality. Nevertheless they provide a reasonably clear baseline for comparison as we move on to consider counter-narratives in the following chapter.

3
Narrating Democracy II

Introduction

The previous chapter outlined the dominant, Schumpeterian narrative of democracy. In this chapter, two lines of analysis are offered: (1) tracing the historical roots of this dominant narrative, and (2) setting out how a range of contemporary critics have challenged that narrative. By covering these themes, we can complete a broad-brush picture of competing narratives of the democratic idea up to about the end of the twentieth century. We can then move on, in chapter 4, to look at new ideas that spin off these narratives, such as ecological or 'green' approaches. I begin with the question of what made Schumpeterianism possible.

How to construct your opponent: Schumpeter and 'the classical model'

As we saw in chapter 2, as a backdrop to his preferred definition of democracy, Schumpeter set up what he called 'the classical doctrine of democracy' so as to knock it down ('ridicule' would not be too strong a word), presenting his new theory as a shining, desirable contrast to the discredited older theory.

Calling it 'the eighteenth-century philosophy of democracy', Schumpeter defined it thus: 'the democratic method is that institutional arrangement for arriving at political decisions which realizes the common good by making the people itself decide issues through the election of individuals who are to assemble in order to carry out its will' ([1943] 1976, 250). This theory, it was argued, was inadequate because (1) there is no such thing as a single conception of the 'common good' upon which all could agree; (2) even if there were, there would still be disputes over how specific issues might best be resolved; and (3), as a consequence, there can be no such thing as a definite 'will of the people'. Elected politicians can neither know the people's will – because there is not one to know – nor trust the people to be rational.

Human nature and politics

Underlying and providing the impetus for all of these arguments against the 'classical model' lay a highly pessimistic view of 'human nature in politics'. Schumpeter grants that people generally may have some reasonable grasp of issues that are of immediate importance (e.g., local issues), especially if they concern their monetary interests. However, it is when we consider issues in 'those regions of national and international affairs that lack a direct and unmistakable link with . . . private concerns, individual volition, command of facts and method of inference soon cease to fulfil the requirements of the classical doctrine.' In such contexts, a 'sense of reality is so completely lost'. The private citizen has no real scope for developing a 'will': 'He is a member of an unworkable committee, the committee of the whole nation, and this is why he expends less disciplined effort on mastering a political problem than he expends on a game of bridge' ([1943] 1976, 261). Insofar as there is a discernible 'popular will' on a subject, Schumpeter worried about it being 'manufactured' in a fashion 'exactly analogous to the ways of commercial advertising' (ibid., 263). And he feared, under the influence of current theories about crowd psychology, that: 'Newspaper readers, radio audiences, members of a party even if not physically gathered together are terribly easy to work up into a psychological crowd and into a state of frenzy in which attempt at rational argument only spurs the animal spirits' (ibid., 257).

Whose 'classical theory'?

That seems clear enough – certainly it is a forthright rejection of the 'classical theory'. Many commentators, however, have had difficulties with this 'classical theory'. It appears to derive from an eccentric jumble of classical sources and writers, enfolding clashing ideas within one blanket conception. Thus, for example, Schumpeter writes explicitly of the 'utilitarians', and specifically Jeremy Bentham, the great nineteenth-century English social and political writer and reformer and founder of the modern idea of *utilitarianism*. The idea of the people deciding through elections, and even the idea of the 'common good', can be linked with Bentham and his followers. At the same time, however, the important idea of the 'general will' or the 'will of the people' is much more commonly (and rightly) associated with the eighteenth-century Swiss-French philosopher Jean-Jacques Rousseau, whose radical ideas about small-scale, communitarian and participatory democracy had a profound influence on thinking in the French Revolution. To put the matter briefly, the so-called classical theory in Schumpeter is an unwieldy, and unconvincing, mismatch of ideas culled from quite different times, places, and social and political contexts.

False foes: Bentham, James Mill and utilitarianism

And a key fact that *this* obscures is that Schumpeter's views – and the subsequent post-Schumpeterian narrative – actually have a good deal in *common* with some of the classical writers whose work he so readily dismisses. The Schumpeterian narrative can be traced back, as well as forward. Consider the views of Bentham and of his chief collaborator, James Mill. These advocates of utilitarianism believed that the role of government was to maximize the utility of individuals, and thus to seek 'the greatest happiness of the greatest number'. The classical utilitarians started with the idea that men are self-seeking, out to maximize their own utility, to maximize their pleasures and to minimize their pains. This is the basis of human nature. Society, therefore, consists of such men (they spoke of men and meant *men*), all seeking to maximize their utility. A key way to try to do this is to gain power over others, since such power can subordinate others to one's will. Having property was also a major source of pleasure – and of power. Crucially, in Bentham and Mill's eyes, members of governments and government officials were just like everyone else – out for their own interests. Clearly this creates a dilemma: all people need the protection of government, so that others may not deny them basic freedoms; but what of government itself depriving citizens of their freedoms? The answer was *representative* government – government which was elected on a regular basis (Bentham favoured annually elected parliaments for England) and thus *accountable* to the people.

Even on this very brief account, we can see the rationale for democracy and the character of – the way of constructing – democracy at work in classical utilitarian thinking. I would point out two of its particular features before mentioning two further precursors of Schumpeterian approaches. First, for the classical utilitarians this was *not* 'democracy'. Even up to around the end of the nineteenth century, 'democracy' standardly meant direct or face-to-face democracy along ancient Athenian lines. Thus James Mill wrote in what is possibly the clearest exposition of classical, Benthamite utilitarianism, 'democracy' is not feasible, since 'all numerous assemblies are essentially incapable of business' (Mill [1861] 1978, 59). Representative government was a combination of the democratic, the aristocratic and the monarchic, designed to act as a restraint on government above all. Second, what could count as 'representation' at that time was distinctive; a rather notorious passage in Mill's 'Essay on Government' pointed out that: 'One thing is pretty clear, that all those individuals whose interests are indisputably included in those of other individuals, may be struck off [the electorate] without inconvenience.' By this logic not only children but also women could be excluded from the franchise, 'the interest of almost all of whom is involved either in that of their fathers or in that of their husbands.'

Protective democracy: back to Locke, and Madison

Bentham and Mill's view of 'democracy' – or, better, representative government – is widely regarded as a paradigm of a 'protective' model of democracy (MacPherson 1977; Held 1996; Pateman 1970). This refers to the fact that they saw the purpose of representative and accountable government to be to *protect* the interests of individuals both from each other and from government itself. This notion of protection resonates considerably with core threads in the Schumpeterian narrative; it also connects Benthamite utilitarianism with very different classic threads in the modern history of the idea of democracy, and I shall comment briefly on Locke and Madison in this context.

The publication of John Locke's *Two Treatises of Government* is widely taken to be a justification of the Glorious Revolution in which William III took the English crown. It is also seen widely as a crucial text in the history of the idea of democracy. As with the classical utilitarians, there is a tremendous range to the ideas and subtleties in Locke's thinking that we do not even touch upon here. For present purposes, the key point is that Locke's influential theory of government was also a *protective* model. Locke saw ideal government as a set of institutions which ruled by consent and by trust. Its origins and justification lay in the fact that all men were naturally free, in a 'state of nature', a stateless existence under God's law alone. But the 'inconveniences' of the state of nature – the arbitrary application of justice, the insecurity of property – led them to *contract* to give up an element of their natural freedom in return for protection, by government, of themselves and their property. So Locke was a *contract* theorist, positing the idea of an original contract to bring into being civil society and with it a government. (To make it clear I do not wish to shoehorn theorists unduly, let me point out that Bentham thought contract theory to be no less than 'nonsense upon stilts', as opposed to the superiority of basic utilitarian assumptions.)

Crucial features arise from the Lockean contract: the idea that government exists to protect pre-existing rights (especially to property); that all legitimate government authority is derived from the consent of the governed; that rebellion could be justified insofar as government betrayed its 'trust' or its rightful role; that it is individuals and their rights that matter which lies at the base of politics; that majority rule ought to be the basic political decision rule; and that accountable government is largely a matter of national level institutional design (to use modern language).

James Madison, the main architect of the political structures of the United States and later the fourth president, was a 'protective' theorist too, profoundly influenced by the arguments of Locke as well as others such as the French Baron Montesquieu. For our purposes, the key to Madison's views lies in *Federalist* paper no. 10. There, he argued strongly that *factions* were inevitable in society; one had to build institutions which dealt with the effects of factional battles, rather than to wish them away. A failure to do so would result in the tyranny of one faction over another. A form of government was required that could protect the interests of all against the ever-present threat of factional tyranny. Madison's response was to make a clear distinction between 'democracy' and a 'republic', and to opt firmly for the *latter*. A democracy, to him, was Athenian-style direct democracy – in essence: 'a society consisting of a small number of citizens, who assemble and administer the government in person'. A republic was 'a government in which the scheme of representation takes place' (quoted in Krouse 1983, 63–4).

Madison was *not* a democrat. His chief concern, in some eyes, was precisely to keep ordinary citizens away from real political influence, and to create a system that could govern a country of continental proportions. He wrote that: 'The two great points of difference between a democracy and a republic are: first, the delegation of the government, in the latter, to a small number of citizens elected by the rest; secondly, the greater number of citizens, and greater sphere of country, over which the latter may be extended' (quoted in Krouse 1983, 64). Here, representation was not a type of democracy, or an institution of democracy. For Madison, it meant 'the total exclusion of the people'.

The notion of representation, however, in the nascent USA, had taken on other meanings. By the 1780s, according to the historian Gordon Wood (1992), representation had come to be seen as something not everyone or anyone could rightly claim to do. Only being *elected* and being responsible to the whole electorate gave you the right to claim to be representative in the political sense. In this way representation came to be seen as 'democratic', since ways of representing (and ways of justifying it) that were more characteristic of monarchical and aristocratic structures of the old world were discredited. At the same time, the original exclusion of the ordinary people from actual running of government was maintained in the new, 'democratic', version of representation.

We are, of course dealing here with a major sweep of history and ideas across countries, continents and eras. My task has been to trace narratives about democracy, to show one or two ways in which conceptions of democracy have been, and can be, constructed. I do not mean to suggest, for example, that all those well-known classical theorists labelled as 'protective' theorists agreed with each other across a range of difficult questions to do with the theory and practice of democracy – of course not. However, past ideas do impact upon recent and present ones (Bentham is, despite Schumpeter's comments, part-author of Schumpeterianism), and present ideas are a prism through which our views of the past can be shaped (Madison reads like a democrat now, since what he *understood* to be anti-democratic has transmogrified into the very essence of a modern democracy).

Making Schumpeterianism possible: an interim summary

That said, let me offer a summary of some key elements we have traced so far. In chapter 2 and above, I have set out some key factors that appeared to form a unifying narrative line through Schumpeter's theory and the works of influential successors. Let me now attempt to show some important ways in which certain classical ideas themselves form the prehistory of that same narrative – how, if you like, certain themes from (e.g.) Locke, Madison, Bentham and James Mill *made Schumpeterianism possible*.

First, recall, Schumpeterian theories were concerned to offer models that were 'realistic' and measurable, and fitted with common assumptions about what 'democracy' meant.

The sense of realism of the classics – Madison and the utilitarians accepting the essentially self-interested nature of people, for example, Locke and Montesquieu likewise in their different ways – provides a precursor to these views. Further, seeing 'democracy' as 'direct democracy', and that in turn as face-to-face Athenian assembly democracy, fostered in these writers a preference for indirect, at best representative forms of politics. Indeed, representation was *not* seen by them as democratic. Though, in the classics, realism meant no or little 'democracy', and for Schumpeterians, it meant *redefining* democracy, we should be aware of the common work that the idea of realism was doing in each case.

Second, the more recent Schumpeterian texts focused very much on the *national* level, concerned above all with the institutional structure of *central* government.

The 'protective' concerns of the selected classic texts that we looked at above led them, arguably, to stress strong, central institutions for developing nation-states; the protector needs to be the strongest force in the land, or else it cannot carry out its defining task properly. Each of the classics we have mentioned was engaged in the machinations of how to divide and unite different branches of government. Most supported the idea of a separation of powers between executive, legislature and judiciary, to make power counteract (Madison) or complement (Mill) power. Lijphart's detailed musings over the differential impacts of varied institutional designs at the centre of national government can be seen as a direct descendant of this work, in particular.

Third, and crucially, the strict focus of Schumpeterianism on indirect or representative government finds powerful underpinnings and forebears in the works of these classical writers.

Each in his own way fears the less-than-rational politics of the mass, and seeks to tame it, sideline it, make it work against itself. We have seen Schumpeter's own views, and we could add to them, for example, the early Dahl's concern to foster 'social training' in the mass of the people in the consensual norms that must underpin a competitive, pluralistic polity (Dahl 1956). In the eighteenth- and nineteenth-century texts, representation is undemocratic; by the mid-twentieth century, it has become the very essence of democracy. Democracy is, and can only be, representative, in the Schumpeterian narrative. The people, however they are constructed or construed, do not have a direct political role to play, and that is to the good. Each of the classic writers is quite clear, too, that democracy is about leadership and leadership selection and election, not popular politics or popular participation.

Fourth, we detected individualism as a key theme in the more recent narrative construction.

If anything, this is even more pronounced, and more insistent, in the classics. Some of the latter reflect and capture moments in the early development of commercial society, with its love of individual freedom (for upper-class white men at any rate), the prime importance of protection of property (this a major and explicit worry of Locke, Madison and the utilitarians) and the broader exaltation of individual rights and happiness. These specific characteristics are what make these theories *liberal* theories. Applying that label to them is important for our purposes because it pinpoints features that one or two important counter-narratives targeted (as we shall see below). The notion of the individual and his self-interest as the essential unit of political life is a powerful product of theories and writings just like those we have noted.

Likewise, *fifth*, democracy was an *instrumental* matter in the classics mentioned here; it was good or useful or desirable not in its own right, not (for example) for the intrinsic benefits of popular participation, but because it tended to produce *something else* of value. The value of representation, for example, lay in its second-order tendency to induce security for property, or non-tyranny in government, or the greatest happiness of the greatest number. Here, in its different ways, democracy is a method or a means, and not really a goal or an end in its own right.

Sixth, the classics do indeed promote an abstract conception of equality – though it does not generally include women, or the poor, or the young, or the enslaved, or people of colour, or indigenous peoples. But this conception of equality *is* formal in nature – it does not, for example, extend to seeing as desirable or necessary broader or substantive notions of economic or social equality. This chimes neatly with the narrower construction of equality in the twentieth-century writers, where political equality for democracy consists in equal rights to a formal vote above all else.

Important narratives have deep historical roots, and I have done no more here than to indicate where some of the roots of Schumpeterian narratives of democracy may be found. There are plenty of discontinuities between key pre-twentieth-century and twentieth-century writers on democracy, too. The classic writers, for example, blended description, attempts at explanation, and normative prescription in distinctive ways; the Schumpeterian line of writers is much more self-consciously descriptive, working within a contemporary conception of what it means to do 'political science'. Nonetheless, I hope enough has been said to suggest where some key traces might be located, and what are some of the building blocks of a highly influential narrative about what democracy may be.

Counterpoints

Critics of Schumpeterian constructions of democracy have come from different traditions. I will canvass briefly the counter-narratives of three groups – participatory democrats, Marxists and feminists. Again, the account will be selective. I mention the work of a small, illustrative group of influential writers in a way that is designed to offer a taste of key counter-narratives of democracy.

Participatory democracy

Let us start with the participatory democrats. These writers – above all, Peter Bachrach (1967), Carole Pateman (1970) and C. B. MacPherson (1977) – between them took aim at each and every aspect of Schumpeter's theory, to construct a counter-narrative built around the desirability of the goal of widespread political participation. Pateman's starting point opened up an alleged gap in Schumpeter's reasoning which created space for such a counter-narrative to take off. Admirers and a number of critics of Schumpeter have, she argues, swallowed uncritically his arguments about the 'classical theory'. But 'what neither its critics nor its defenders have realized is that *the notion of "a classical theory of democracy" is a myth*' (1970, 17, italics in the original). One key reason for this fact is that Schumpeter 'has not realized that two very different theories about democracy are to be found' in so-called classical writings (1970, 18). One theory, that of Bentham, for example, actually supports many Schumpeterian assumptions, as we saw from the brief discussion above; another one, centred on other classical authors Rousseau and John Stuart Mill, offers a quite different, participatory orientation.

So, according to this view, Schumpeter's black-and-white, classical-versus-modern construction papers over compelling alternatives, which the critics now bring to light and develop. (Note that Pateman locates just *two* classical theories – we can expect an argumentative strategy of one-bad-one-good, the good ignored by Schumpeter because it does not support what he says. On all sides, narrative-construction shoehorns traditions, texts and events to tighten and define the story.) In the 1960s through to the 1980s, threads of the participatory democracy critique were disputed and elaborated; in a range of ways, arguments were put forward which countered Schumpeterian claims. I review four such arguments briefly here.

What realism hides   First, participationists took aim at the claim of 'realism', and related concerns, to be descriptive or positive rather than normative. Bachrach wrote that, although 'elitist democratic theory' (as he called it) aimed to offer *explanations*, in reality it was 'deeply rooted in an ideology, an ideology which is grounded upon a profound distrust of the majority of ordinary men and women, and a reliance upon the established elites' (1967, 93). Similarly, MacPherson locates in the Benthamite roots of Schumpeterianism a significant lack of enthusiasm for democracy, and 'no idea that it could be a morally transformative force', since it is painted as 'nothing but a logical requirement for the governance of inherently self-interested conflicting individuals who are assumed to be infinite desirers of their own private benefits' (1977, 43).

In short, the allegation is that the 'realism' was selective and prejudiced. Insofar as their definitions of democracy were attuned to their 'realism' and their desire to describe democracy as it was in the real world, they could be accused of ignoring important, normative and participative features of democracy by lowering their sights to what *is*, and by applauding the latter. Of course, the Schumpeterian view was all about avoiding value judgements that get in the way of proper social scientific analysis. But this is not such an easy thing to do – fences built between the explanatory and the normative keep getting holes punched in them. As another critic, Quentin Skinner, put it: 'the underlying impression of political conservatism . . . is generated by the fact that the existing, operative political system is commended implicitly, through the equation between its salient features and the allegedly sufficient conditions for saying of a political system that it is genuinely a democracy' (Skinner 1973, 301). Not content simply to point out what they saw as the deeper normative roots of their opponents' surface neutrality, the participatory democrats were unashamedly normative; in their view, democracy was not simply a means to some other end, *but a goal or ideal in itself.* It was viewed by them as a project that was never complete but which always carried more practical potential to further engage the interest, encourage the participation, and develop the personal capacities and confidence of ordinary citizens.

Extending democracy's scope   Second, all participatory democrats contested the view that 'democracy' was only relevant to national politics and the shaping of national political institutions and procedures. They argued that democracy could (and should) be practised in many places or sites, and be a part of many decision-making processes *outside* the state or government as well as inside it. They were interested in the democratization of society, not just of the state. Indeed, the participatory democrats largely accepted that, as Bachrach put it, 'the exigencies of life in the industrial and nuclear age necessitate that key and crucial political decisions in a democracy, as in totalitarian societies, would be made by a handful of men [*sic*]' (1967, 1); and Pateman wrote that:

'in an electorate of, say, thirty-five millions the role of the individual must consist almost entirely of choosing representatives' (1970, 109). But the scope for instituting and practising democracy in varied sites and organizations of civil society beyond the state was considerable. Different participatory theorists championed and elaborated upon different sites. Bachrach wrote, though briefly and sketchily, of the role that democracy within factories could play in his preferred 'self-developmental model of democracy' (1967, 100, 103). A good proportion of Pateman's key text is devoted to the possibility of democracy and participation in industry. Spheres such as industry, she argued, 'should be seen as political systems in their own right, offering areas of participation additional to the national level' (1970, 43).

MacPherson proposed a model of participatory democracy with particular focus on the potential to institute a bottom-up, pyramidal structure of participation within *political parties*: 'The combination of a pyramidal direct/indirect democratic machinery with a continuing party system seems essential. Nothing but a pyramidal system will incorporate any direct democracy into a nationwide structure of government, and some significant amount of direct democracy is required for anything that can be called participatory democracy' (1977, 112). Actual developments, in the USA and in Europe, for example, were in line with some of these prescriptions; reforms aimed at democratizing the selection of the presidential candidate in the US Democratic Party in the early 1970s, changes that gave greater power to trade unions and constituencies in the Labour Party in the UK, and grassroots democracy innovations in the German Green Party in the 1980s are key instances.

Indeed, 'participation' was a widespread goal into the 1970s in Western countries, reflecting and spawning significant events and innovations such as the famous 'war on poverty' of the Johnson years and after in the USA, and the reforms of the National Health Service in Britain that led to the creation of patients' and citizens' bodies within the system. Further participatory theorists, such as Barber (1984), discussed in detail the possibilities for renewing participatory democracy in local community politics. Citizen participation in the running of local, and local branches of national, institutions such as schools and hospitals were of great interest too. The participatory democracy narrative, generally speaking, stressed a broad, society-wide conception of 'politics' and a flexible and open attitude to which processes and institutions of society as well as the state could foster the benefits of grassroots participation in decision-making. As part of the same point, it will be evident from the brief remarks here that the Schumpeterian focus on strictly *representative* forms of democracy – and consequently on elections as the primary democratic mechanism – was subject to participatory criticism. Democracy could and should be about direct popular participation in a variety of sites and processes, as well as national-level representative processes.

Citizens and their capabilities The conception of the individual that lay at the heart of so many orthodox accounts of representative democracy was, as we have seen, based on assumptions of a self-interested, self-contained, individual. This individual had his ('she' never figured) preferences or desires, and these were taken as more-or-less 'given'. Schumpeter, for example, was much more doubtful about the capacities and rationality of ordinary people than a precursor such as Bentham (in theory at least, and as long as women are not included), but the general point holds. The participatory theorists constructed a very different view of individuals and their actual and potential capacities. Bachrach was keen to add a new purpose, a new goal, to the orthodox Schumpeterian theory of democracy, namely that of the development of citizens. There was no need to take an unduly narrow or fixed view of what constituted peoples' interests. Why could we not also see as intrinsic to somebody's interests 'the opportunity for development which accrues from participation in meaningful political decisions' (Bachrach 1967, 95)? Pateman was concerned primarily with the educative effects of participation: the sense of efficacy that stood to be gained by individuals taking advantage of opportunities for genuine participation in decisions affecting their lives. Further benefits would accrue at the level of the larger system if particular or local opportunities for participation were fostered, not least social integration and the acceptability of decisions. She wrote: 'One might characterize the participatory model as one where maximum input (participation) is required and where output includes not just policies (decisions) but also the development of the social and political capacities of each individual' (1970, 43). In short, individuals were not pre-packed bundles of fixed preferences and fixed propensities; they possessed potential that could be nurtured and shaped, for their benefit and for that of their societies, if it were to be fostered by taking up opportunities for political participation in the workplace, in their local communities, within parties and interest groups, and so on.

A broader view of equality   Finally, it is worth noting that participatory theorists were concerned in part about extending the spheres of politics and democracy because they regarded social and economic equality as important to democracy, in addition to narrower views of political equality in the form of equal votes of equal value. In the context of her advocacy of workers' participation in industry, for example, Pateman writes of 'the substantive measure of economic equality required to give the individual the independence and security necessary for equal participation; the democratizing of industrial authority structures, abolishing the permanent distinction between "managers" and "men" would mean a large step toward meeting this condition' (1970, 43).

The participatory counter-narrative: an interim summary

We must not exaggerate either the similarities or discontinuities sketched here. For example, Bachrach and other participatory theorists largely swallow the 'classical myth' that Schumpeter bequeathed to post-war democratic theory. Pateman shares a concern for social and system integration at the macro level with the Dahl of *A Preface to Democratic Theory*. And none of the major participatory theorists questioned basically Schumpeterian arguments about how national-level democracy would need to be organized and conducted in large-scale modern states. Nonetheless, the participatory democracy critique adds up to a distinctive narrative of democracy in its own right.

So, in brief, over about a twenty-year period there built up a reasonably comprehensive participative counter-narrative to the Schumpeterian orthodoxy in democratic theory. Like the Schumpeterian view, and indeed like any effort to construct a narrative with some claim to internal coherence, the participatory version had its blind spots, its special concerns and focus, its assumptions. Setting these aside, key elements included:

- the educative, 'developmental' function of participation;
- the view that democracy was an ideal, a goal worthy of continuously deeper levels of achievement;
- a broad understanding of 'politics' and of 'democracy', stretching the meanings of both terms beyond the confines of national state institutions to encompass a variety of sites of desirable and potential democratization across modern societies;
- the inappropriateness of the market model for politics, a model that posits individuals with fixed preferences and motivations, and a preference for a progressive, developmental view; and
- the fact that, behind its 'descriptive' and 'realistic' veneer, the orthodox narrative was value-laden or normative in favouring implicitly what exists over what might be, and with it the real over the ideal.

The classical roots of participatory democracy

This participatory counter-narrative had its classical roots, too. Pateman, most clearly and explicitly, referred back to Rousseau and John Stuart Mill to excavate what Schumpeterian orthodoxy had buried (in her view): a developmental, participative thread in key works of important, influential classical writers. I shall not examine Rousseau and Mill here in this context, beyond the following brief comments (the reader is invited to follow this up independently). John Stuart Mill, writing in *Representative Government* in particular, feared for the stability of government and society in England if the extension of the democratic franchise was not accompanied by efforts to encourage the taking of responsibility and the moderating of views and habits by lower-class men, newly arrived in the class of voters. In that context he extolled the virtues of participation in certain types of local decision-making for its educative, developmental effects. He saw local government as an appropriate training ground where ordinary people could participate and benefit. Pateman understands that, for Mill, 'it is at the local level where the real educative effect of participation occurs, where not only do the issues dealt with directly affect the individual and his everyday life but where he also stands a good chance of, himself, being elected to serve on a local body' (1970, 31).

Similarly, going back further, Pateman took from Rousseau the idea that participation has educative effects for the individuals who do the participating. Rousseau's pre-French Revolutionary vision of the ideal polity in his *Social Contract* seems, at first, to have little relevance to modern efforts to understand democracy. He envisions a small, face-to-face, rural society run in accordance with the 'general will', a conception of the common good which encompasses all community members and in the making of which they all participate. Sovereignty – the basic power base of the community – cannot be alienated or represented, and so it rests with the people. This is a vision of direct, not representative, politics. However – and this is often a source of confusion – Rousseau did not envision ordinary citizens actually carrying out the administrative and other tasks of government. Understanding *that* as 'democracy' for his purposes, he famously wrote that democracy was for Gods, not men. Yet he conveyed a particularly strong sense of civic duty and obligation, and the central importance of participation in fostering and maintaining this: 'In a well-ordered city', he wrote, 'every man flies to the assemblies' (Rousseau [1762] 1973, 240).

The (ir)relevance of ancient Athens?

I have said little about 'direct democracy' here. Most of the participatory democrats have little to say about it too – they see 'participatory democracy' as a *broader* category of political empowerment than simply having direct votes on issues in formal governmental processes, national or local. There are partial exceptions to this – note MacPherson on 'direct' elements of potential pyramidal structures, above – and more full-blooded ones, such as Barber's advocacy of local, face-to-face, decision-making assemblies and the use of referendums (more on that in chapter 5). As a result, perhaps, little is said about ancient Athens, where democracy was 'invented' as 'direct democracy'.[1]

The dismissal of Athenian experience as irrelevant to modern politics from a dominant-narrative perspective is most forthright in the work of Giovanni Sartori, a leading democratic theorist and critic of the 'participatory' school of thought. Sartori writes that 'ancient democracies cannot teach us anything about building a democratic state and about conducting a democratic system that covers not merely a small city but a larger expanse of territory inhabited by a vast collectivity' (1987, 2.279). Others, however, have found in Athenian practice a source of criticism of Schumpeterian assumptions and aspirations, despite the chronological and cultural gulf separating Athens and twentieth-century Western democracies. In particular, Moses Finley finds resources that undergird claims about popular inclusion and the educative effects of participation:

> it would be absurd to make any direct comparison with a small, homogenous, face-to-face society such as Athens; absurd to suggest, even to dream, that we might reinstate an Assembly of the citizens as the paramount decision-making body in a modern city or nation . . . Public apathy and political ignorance are a fundamental fact today, beyond any possible dispute; decisions are made by political leaders, not by popular vote, which at best has only an occasional veto power after the fact. The issue is whether this state of affairs is, under modern conditions, a necessary and desirable one, or whether new forms of popular participation, in the Athenian spirit though not in the Athenian substance, if I may phrase it that way, need to be invented. (Finley 1985, 36)

The spirit of Athens that Finley would have us foster in new institutions would reflect a feature of Athenian politics that was 'an astounding novelty in its time, rarely repeated thereafter', namely the incorporation into full membership of the political community 'peasants, shopkeepers and craftsmen who were citizens alongside the educated upper classes' (1985, 16). Of course, as the warnings of both Sartori and Finley remind us, the small, rural, face-to-face, non-liberal, slave-owning and exclusive polity (women, slaves and foreigners could not be 'citizens') of fourth- and fifth-century BC Athens allows no easy extrapolations to today's politics. But at the margins at least, the participatory narrative embraced 'Athens' as the embodiment of a spirit that stood in stark contrast to the perceived poverty of aspiration, and distrust of ordinary citizens, that Schumpeterian orthodoxy seemed to convey. From this angle, simply to say, as Sartori does, 'all our democracies are indirect' (1987, 2.180) rather begs the question: are they, then, as fully 'democratic' as they might be, and is it impossible that genuinely direct elements could not supplement the necessarily indirect ones? When considering innovations in direct democracy in chapter 5, I shall return to the potential usefulness of mechanisms common to ancient Athens in today's politics.

The participatory democracy narrative was aligned with the politics of student protest against the Vietnam War in the USA and the UK in particular in the 1960s and the 1970s. This movement, along with others expressing solidarity with third-world liberation movements, for example, gave rise to new and renewed ideas about state, society and democracy on the political left. At various points, Marxist and feminist criticisms of liberal democratic orthodoxy overlap with the participatory critique; we deal here with cases of intertwining narratives and complex intertextuality – not least because some academic authors charted the way through compatible elements of different narratives (Carole Pateman was, and is, a leading participatory theorist and feminist theorist, for example). Keeping this fact in mind, let us look finally at further narratives with distinctive takes on prevailing ideas about democracy in the post-war period in particular, beginning with Marxism.

Marxist critiques

There are many 'Marxisms', some of which broke from the unthinking, jargonistic Soviet and Chinese orthodoxies in the

1950s and 1960s to provoke debate about the adequacy of standard Western conceptions of democracy, and what the latter 'left out'. To fix our bearings, let us draw on Gregor McLennan's claim that three propositions must form the core of any Marxist theory of the state: (1) Western societies are based on capitalist economies, involving class divisions and economic exploitation and inequality; (2) the state's role is to ensure the stability of capitalist society; its actions favour capitalist enterprises; and (3) modern pluralist democracy is *bourgeois democracy*, narrow and individualistic, serving sectional interests rather than the common interest (McLennan 1990). Influential Marxist theorists such as Louis Althusser, Ralph Miliband and Nicos Poulantzas picked up important threads from the work of the Italian theorist and political leader Antonio Gramsci, in particular, to attempt to demonstrate the bogus nature of the existing liberal democracies and the inadequacy of their supporting theories. It is worth pausing for a moment to look at Gramsci's ideas.

Consent and coercion: Gramsci's Marxism Antonio Gramsci was an Italian politician and theorist whose writing on capitalism and the state in the 1920s and 1930s from within one of Mussolini's prisons challenged Marxist–Leninist dogmatism and, after World War II, helped to spawn less sectarian 'Eurocommunist' parties in Western Europe (in Italy, Spain and France in particular). Gramsci's major contribution to political thought on the left was to emphasize the role of ideological, political and moral factors in the domination of one social class by another. For many political analysts, he provided a novel and powerful lens through which to view the twin processes of consent and coercion in the Western democratic state.

His distinctive focus on *hegemony* or domination in his *Prison Notebooks* (1971) sets Gramsci's work apart from the Marxist–Leninist orthodoxy. In Marx and Engels's most famous account, the state was merely 'superstructural', a reactive set of institutions whose shape and role was essentially determined by society's economic structure (or base); in the words of the *Communist Manifesto*, 'the executive of the modern state is but a committee for managing the common affairs of the whole bourgeoisie.' The importance of the 'base–superstructure' model within Marxism was reinforced by Lenin, who emphasized the class-ridden nature and the repressive functions of the capitalist, supposedly 'democratic', state.

Confronted by the triumph of Fascism over socialism in Italy, Gramsci came to regard the state in a different light (though there is little doubt that he always saw himself as an orthodox Marxist). To his mind, the effective domination of the capitalist class over the working class was a product of something more than simply repression or coercion via the state. It also required the *consent* of the dominated to the terms of their own domination. It is the role of consent, and of the institutions through which such consent is obtained, that lies at the heart of the idea of hegemony.

For Gramsci, the modern state consisted of more than just executive, legislative and judicial institutions. In effect, he argued, there exists an extended state, made up of organizations not normally thought of as being part of the state, such as the church, trade unions, orthodox political parties, the schools and universities, and the media. As he put it in his *Prison Notebooks*, Gramsci felt that 'The state should be understood not only as the apparatus of government, but also the private apparatus of hegemony or civil society.' His central point was that these civil institutions played a key role in winning over the hearts and minds of working-class people to that order. Hence, in Gramsci's equation, 'State = political society + civil society, in other words hegemony protected by the armour of coercion.' From a Gramscian perspective, the trick for the ruling class in capitalist societies is to pass off its particularistic ideology as received wisdom or common sense, and in that way avoid the need for overt coercion.

His views concerning hegemony moulded Gramsci's outlook as a political strategist. Capitalist hegemony in the West requires countervailing sources of hegemony – ideas crafted by an independent moral and intellectual leadership to oppose the received wisdom of the existing order in a flexible and subtle manner. Reflecting his earlier sponsorship of workers' factory councils, Gramsci stressed the need for the left to build, piece by piece, a new hegemonic force to oppose dominant ideology and dominant institutions alike.

We can see in Gramsci's Marxism a deep suspicion of orthodox claims to 'democracy' along Schumpeterian lines, and a concern with sites of participation and empowerment which overlaps with that of participatory democrats. The main difference is that Marxists like Gramsci do not accept as legitimate existing state structures and the representative politics attached to them, whereas the participatory democrats largely did so. Marxists argue that, underneath the apparent competition and pluralism that authors such as Schumpeter and Dahl (in different texts and modes) emphasized, there is a unity of purpose which revolves around a ruling class defending its privileges.

Neo-Gramscian and other radical critiques Althusser, Miliband and Poulantzas built on Gramsci's critique in the 1960s to the 1980s. Althusser (1971) stressed the ways in which there is a deep objective structure of class domination underlying all surface appearances of pluralistic and 'democratic' politics, and in which all individuals are 'bearers' or 'carriers' of this structure. He also emphasized how ruling-class ideology was reinforced and deepened by the workings of what he called Ideological State Apparatuses (e.g., schools, the media, the family). Miliband took a more empirical and sociological view of the role of the state, stressing the common social background of economic, social and political elites, and their consequent favouring of certain sectional interests in society over others, above all big business interests.

It is worth noting too that non-Marxist radical democratic critiques made similar points against the dominant democratic narrative. Charles Lindblom, writing in *Politics and Markets* in 1977, for example, wrote that business's 'privileged position' has major consequences for polyarchy (recall the features of polyarchy, discussed above): 'the systems we call polyarchies operate under two groups of leaders. But only one of them is systematically subject to polyarchal control' (1977, 189). And, like Lindblom, Robert Dahl in the 1980s re-established himself as a radical critic of democratic orthodoxies, arguing that, to extend and deepen polyarchy or democracy, modern capitalist societies should have a system of cooperatively self-governing enterprises (for example, in which employees choose managers and collectively own the enterprise). To back this view up, Dahl contended that, 'If democracy is justified in governing the state, then it is also justified in governing economic enterprises. What is more, if it cannot be justified in governing economic enterprises, we do not quite see how it can be justified in governing the state' (1985, 134–5).

In short: Marxist and radical counter-narratives emphasized:

- the class context of democratic politics;
- the fact that democracy centrally involves coercion as well as consent;
- that people might 'consent' to systems of rule, leaders and policies that are not in fact in their real interests; and
- that 'democratic' societies normally contain deep and lasting economic and social inequalities.

I turn now to the final major counter-narrative, that of feminism.

Feminist critiques

Feminist critiques of the state and liberal democracy had various targets. For one thing, they argued, both pre-twentieth-century classic works and the Schumpeterians side-lined women, sometimes explicitly and sometimes implicitly, sometimes deliberately and sometimes out of habit. We saw how Schumpeter and Downs made passing references to 'pretty girls' and 'cigarettes' and 'democracies' in which women were not allowed to vote; Dahl in 1956 had an example of 'Jones' preferring 'blondes to brunettes' in illustrating issues of intensity of preference in democratic theory. In some of the classics we find the place of women more starkly and deliberately set out. James Mill happily excluded women from the need to vote, as we saw. Rousseau took a dim view of the role of women, writing, for example, that 'Woman is especially made for man's delight', and 'Unable to judge for themselves, they should accept the judgement of father and husband as that of the church' (quoted in Levin 1992, 180). All of these examples might be regarded as trivial throwaway comments, but I would maintain they reflect a mindset that underpins the discriminatory use of 'men' to describe all political participants. Just as there are many Marxisms, so there are many feminisms. On the issues at hand, however, most contemporary feminists would agree that a set of pernicious patriarchal (or male-dominated) assumptions running through mainstream writings about democracy serve systematically to downgrade the roles, capacities and status of women in democratic ideas and practices.

Feminist political critiques in recent years have been targeted especially at the patriarchal and therefore fundamentally inegalitarian features of liberal and democratic aspects of modern politics in the West. According to feminist narratives, the foundations of liberal democracy in mainstream political theory since the seventeenth century have been (1) individualism and individual rights, (2) limited government, and (3) the public/private dichotomy. In theory, liberalism is neutral between all 'individuals', regardless of sex or class; rights are universal and can be deployed to challenge assumptions about natural inferiority.

The core of feminism is the critique of the public/private dichotomy. This dichotomy, or distinction, they argue, has served to make women 'disappear' from the realm of political ideas, confining their role to the domestic sphere. The independent, choice-making individual of classical liberal theory is constructed to fit attributes widely held to be male, and opposed to those held to be characteristic of women. Referring to the dichotomy between public and domestic spheres, feminists argue that the 'public' sphere (state and civil society) often continues to be understood as the sphere of *culture*, of *men*, of *independence*, of *rationality*, and of *citizenship* through *civil* and *political* rights. The private or domestic sphere, by contrast, is defined in terms of *nature*, *women*, *dependence*, *instinct*, *uncertain citizenship* status and *social* rights. In this way, feminists maintain that the apparently neutral public/private dichotomy is in fact biased towards men's interests, and represents patriarchal ideology.

Key feminist concerns arising from the critique of the public/private dichotomy which have an impact on the dominant, Schumpeterian narrative include:

- persisting under-representation of women in the public sphere of paid work and politics: formal electoral democracy embodies equality (one person, one vote, for example), but arguably it misses or even preserves larger social inequalities;

- the view that 'the personal is political', i.e., that the domestic sphere involves power relations and therefore political relations, and thus that democracy should also be about what happens there and not just within state institutions;
- the view that the social preconditions for exercising civil and political rights – and therefore for full citizenship – are not taken seriously by liberal democrats, a view with a direct impact on women's opportunities and status in the public sphere; underlying inequalities of opportunity have an impact on people's opportunities to play the polyarchal game; and
- the assertion that liberal individualism masks the needs of *groups*, such as women.

To make these points is not to suggest that there are easy or uncontroversial ways to address feminist concerns about orthodox views of democracy. Instituting state recognition of housework, or systematic state provision of child care, for example, in order to address some larger social inequalities in democratic societies, may bring its own problems in turn. Rather, the feminist critique underscores the view that the mainstream democratic narrative is narrow and ignores a great deal that any democrat ought not ignore.

I also do not suggest that feminist counter-narratives involve a wholesale rejection of all key elements in the dominant narrative. Many feminists seek to retain liberal democracy and improve it, rather than adopt new models (such as some radical versions of participatory democracy) which carry new dangers. A favoured strategy is to use the liberal democratic notions of rights, etc., to criticize liberal democratic practice with regard to women. Further, the idea of a private sphere is not opposed in principle; the objection, rather, is where the line is drawn and how it is understood.

Conclusion

This chapter, like chapter 2, has examined key narratives of democracy. We have seen how at various points the threads of different narratives have frayed at the edges – as inevitably they will. We have built on some of the key questions which emerged from the open discussion in chapter 1, in that (1) further evidence of the richness of democracy as a signifier is supplied by the debate covered here; (2) the issue of 'political units' within national states (factories, localities) was canvassed; and (3) further institutional resources with which to address design issues such as the problem of 'country X' arose from Schumpeterian and alternative narratives.

I reiterate the warning that we have only skimmed the surface of many of the texts discussed in these chapters; there is no substitute for further reading in this respect. The same goes for key elements of the historical, cultural and social context out of which the authors of these texts crafted their ideas. Nevertheless, with these narratives sketched, we are in a position to move on in chapter 4 to consider the potential impact on familiar lines of democratic narrative of present and future challenges, such as environmentalism and globalization. These are challenges to *all* the narratives or models of democracy considered above: late twentieth- and early twenty-first-century dilemmas and opportunities to rethink democracy for a new era. 'Globalization', for example, would seem to require a radical rethinking of how the nation-state has dominated democratic thinking in *each* of the narratives we have canvassed in this and the previous chapter. The growth in ecological consciousness, too, seems to demand a deepening of conceptions of 'interests' to cover longer-term concerns of people and the real interests of non-human animals and even of ecosystems – something similarly not to be found in *any* of the narratives looked at so far. Looking at examples like these in the following chapter should put us in a position in chapter 5 to see how some of the most prominent new innovations in thinking about democracy might address today's major challenges, and in so doing to build up *new* narratives that variously draw upon and reject elements of those we have examined thus far.

4

Five Challenges

Introduction

The overall focus of this book is, of course, the *idea* of democracy, which means that it is about theories, perspectives and approaches as much as specific institutions (such as elections). Previous chapters have uncovered troubling issues about the definition of democracy, and how some leading twentieth-century narratives of democracy addressed (or failed to address) some of those issues. Perennial concerns about the meaning and the demands of democracy persist; in this chapter we add some new ones to the list. I mentioned at the beginning of the book the idea of 'dipping' into selected problems and cases as a way of introducing debates on the idea of democracy. In that spirit, this chapter focuses on five selected contemporary challenges, many of them specific to uncertainties and problems of the political world in the early twenty-first century. The intention, as in earlier chapters, is to explore the contours of these challenges, and not to prescribe or to attempt ready answers to the dilemmas they pose.

The five challenges dealt with here are as follows:

1   How can we specify *boundaries* to the interpretation of democracy? Can it be just anything?   This issue loomed

large, of course, from our discussions of the cases in chapter 1, especially when considering General Musharraf's 'democratic' claims in the Pakistani case. Presumably, the buck must stop somewhere – if democracy can mean anything, then effectively it will mean nothing.

2 What is the impact of *globalization* upon democracy? 'Globalization' tends to be used in multiple and often contradictory ways. But insofar as it refers to the importance of new centres of political power which are not states (regional institutions like those of the European Union, and international and global ones like the United Nations and the World Trade Organization), it raises issues about the possible need for new forms of democratic control and accountability.

3 How can democracy cope with increasing organizational and policy *complexity* in the contemporary state. The bulk of the views of democracy canvassed in chapters 2 and 3 talked of the link between elected politicians and 'the people'. But what of the vast bureaucracy – administrative, judicial and regulatory bodies – which makes up the modern state? States do more than ever before, and the levels of expertise required are greater than ever, raising a range of questions about the possibility of democracy today.

4 What dilemmas does *environmentalism* pose for democratic ideas and practices? Environmentalists question a great deal of received wisdom about democracy. Can democratic politics encompass the interests of non-human nature? Have democratic systems adapted effectively to the environmentalist wave?

5 Do the prospects for democracy differ in Western and in non-Western contexts? We think of democracy as being something of universal value. Certainly this was the view of Amartya Sen, for example, who was cited in chapter 1. But is democracy a Western liberal idea, not a universal one? Is it flexible and appealing enough to be judged necessary and desirable in all countries and cultures?

Again, for the most part I confine myself in this chapter to outlining the nature of the challenges. In chapter 5, we will look at some innovative new ideas about democracy, many of which have been offered as a *response* to these challenges – for example, ecological or 'green' efforts to rethink democracy as a response to environmental challenges showing up alleged 'blind spots' in the conventional models.

Constructing the scales of democracy

We saw in chapter 1 that 'democracy' can and does signify many things. Many political scientists are engaged in the task of seeking agreed definitions of democracy along with a common scale for measuring it. The need to be sensitive to democracy's different possibilities and meanings in different places and cultures, however, makes it a highly challenging task. There are plenty of writers on democracy who have responded by offering clear ideas as to what counts as democracy and what does not. But nobody's ideas are neutral or beyond contest. My task here is to sketch briefly some key elements of this challenge.

Threshold and continuum

Let us distinguish, first, between the ideas of a *threshold* standard, on the one hand, and a *continuum*, on the other. Specifying a threshold standard can help us to understand what is a democracy and what is not. For example, one might argue that a country is a democracy if it has had a specified period of experience of free and fair elections at the national level (and that it is not a democracy if it has not). The threshold is the boundary between democracy and non-democracy. The continuum, on the other hand, deals with *how much* democracy is present in a country (or other unit). How far above the bare minimum of satisfying the threshold standard does a country's democratic practice go? For example, one might say that the extent to which people enjoy rights to freedom of assembly and speech, and the extent to which the courts are free of patronage or corruption, are important in determining how far above the threshold a given country's democratic system might be 'placed'.

Rhetoric and substance

To say the least, there are different ways of constructing and deploying threshold and continuum standards. To think about some issues involved, let's go back briefly to the case discussion in chapter 1, where we ended up with a variety of possible meanings for democracy after looking at the ways in which it was invoked in the focused case studies. The list included, for example, the importance of *votes counting in fair elections*, on the one hand, and *'doing what is right' politically*, on the other. As a first step towards distinguishing among the entries on that list, with the reasonable boundaries of democracy in mind, I would recommend in particular a distinction between entries that are more *rhetorical and subjective*, on the one hand, and those that are more *substantial and verifiable*, on the other. With specific reference to the discussion in chapter 1, it is difficult to *verify* any claim that a leader is acting in the national interest, or 'doing the right thing' (see the list on p. 13). All we really have to go on is the *claim* itself. Such claims are sometimes easy to make, precisely because it is so difficult for anyone else to contradict them decisively. Whether or not the claims are 'true' is in the end a rather subjective matter. A military dictator, for instance, who came to power through force rather than through popular choice, can *claim* readily enough to be acting in the national interest, to be doing the right thing for his people, and so on. But unless there is some consistent, clear and fair mechanism by which the people can express *their* views on what is in their interests, or decide who can speak in their name, the claim may appear hollow and lacking in supporting evidence. If a claim is not satisfactorily verified by the operation of some mechanism or device or institution that can show it to be justified, then we may be led to conclude that it is almost entirely rhetorical – hot air and no substance.

Other possible meanings *do* seem to offer at least the possibility of comparing institutional features of political systems. Consider in this light certain other possible meanings arising from our cases in chapter 1: fair votes in open and fair elections, the choices of the people prevailing, collective self-government by local and national communities, and the role of proper rules and procedures. Of course, just what each of these means, and what each might demand of us in different contexts, can be a matter of legitimate dispute. However, these features do appear to go beyond rhetoric or extreme subjectivity; without reasonably open elections taking place, then it will be difficult for political figures to maintain that the choices of the people have prevailed, for example. It will not always be easy, and it is far from a wholly objective matter, to gauge how freely and fairly elections have been conducted – witness the events and debates around Florida in 2000, discussed in chapter 1 – but in principle such matters are subject to reasonable verification.

Democracy's meaning

Further, and taking a more general view, these features from the cases from chapter 1 taken together appear to express democracy as a system in which: (a) a certain degree of *political equality and fairness* needs to be instituted tangibly; (b) the credibility or acceptability of policies and actions depends on them being the product of *popular power* in some tangible sense; and (c) basic procedures are more-or-less *transparent*, open to public scrutiny. Equality and fairness, popular power and transparency: I do not propose this as a *definition* of democracy; I would, however, put these principles forward as necessary *ingredients* or *components* of a reasonable definition of democracy. If any of them are *not* part of a definition of democracy, or are not at least *implied by* a definition, then I suggest that we would have reason to suspect that definition to be partial. Although democracy's meaning is constructed and open to legitimate contestation, I am suggesting that a construction of 'democracy' that offers little beyond rhetoric and extreme subjectivity, and does not in some tangible way embrace equality or fairness, popular power and transparency, will be incomplete or inadequate.

(Incidentally, in my view this does not *necessarily* rule out all of the claims of General Musharraf that we encountered in chapter 1. *Local* as well as national elections and fairness and transparency count, too, and if his encouragement of local democracy is genuine it *might* balance to a degree the impact of his coup displacing elected leaders at the national level. Let me make it clear that a very much fuller study of this case would be needed – perhaps the kind of study a good political anthropologist might carry out, since anthropologists are very sensitive to local context in a way that I have advocated – before even tentative conclusions along these lines could reasonably be reached. As I emphasized throughout chapter 1 and elsewhere, I do not pass judgement on these cases, but rather I use them to help sharpen our thinking about democracy's possible meanings.)

Dilemmas in measuring democracy

Political scientists face various awkward dilemmas in their efforts to construct appropriate scales for the detection and measurement of democracy. Do they concentrate on 'democracy or not', black-and-white issues (a threshold standard), or do they try to construct continuous measures (a continuum)? Do they use objective indicators (e.g., electoral turnout), subjective ones (e.g., degrees of individual freedom), or some combination? Should there be individual judges of 'democraticness', or is a panel of experts better? And should there be measures at a single time, or over time?[1] Whatever the precise answers to these questions, it is evident that experts need to establish *control* over their object, to *construct* it in particular ways, in order to scale and measure it; and there will always be credible grounds on which to challenge the particular slant evident in their strategies for control and construction of 'democracy'. It would seem that the best approach to constructing scales for democracy would be one which is sensitive to difference, variation, the need for flexibility in measures and interpretations alike. Particular experiences in real, specific places matter. Simple lists of countries that are 'democratic' or 'partially democratic' or 'undemocratic' almost always hide or gloss over features of countries that provide a much more subtle and complex picture in reality.

In this context, the work of Beetham (1994) is particularly instructive. In order to conduct a 'democratic audit' of the

UK, Beetham constructed measures of democracy in the form of *questions* covering accountability, elections, rights and civil society. Some questions lent themselves to more quantitative, objective answers (though of course these still require subjective interpretation). Others involved more subjective and qualitative interpretation. Beetham and his colleagues have refused to consider an overall 'score' for democracy, instead breaking down his scales and questions into sub-areas and sub-principles 'which go to make up the major dimensions of democracy for contemporary societies' (such as 'open and accountable government', and 'free and fair elections') (Beetham 1994, 30). I will not elaborate further here, but simply say that the 'democratic audit' project (a) exhibits to a considerable degree concerns about sensitivity to shifting and alternative meanings, and the need to deploy scales which are sensitive to context, and (b) deploys as basic principles *political equality* and *popular control*, a similar set to that we arrived at tentatively on the basis of our considerations in earlier chapters.

Overall, then, my response regarding this first challenge is that there are boundaries to the reasonable interpretation of democratic principles (and therefore of democracy), but that the precise nature and location of those boundaries is dynamic, and not a fixed affair. Democracy, along with its core principles of political equality, popular power and transparency, can mean different things in different (and even the same) contexts, but it cannot mean just anything, anywhere.

The challenge of globalization

We turn now to a larger challenge (or threat?). Globalization, a complex process whereby (it is argued) nation-states are becoming increasingly interconnected and interdependent, poses a variety of pressing questions for the practice and theory of democracy. Almost inevitably, globalization is a term that means different things to different people. To the protesters who voiced their grievances regarding world poverty and inequality at summit meetings of world leaders from Seattle to Prague to Quebec City to Genoa in the years

2000 and 2001, it has meant large and powerful transnational companies, facilitated by international regulatory bodies such as the World Trade Organization (WTO), becoming increasingly dominant over national governments and the ordinary people subject to them. To its supporters, globalization means, for example, extending international free trade so that all countries can participate in and benefit economically and otherwise from it. It is not simply an economic phenomenon, but rather one with important political, social and cultural features too.

Trends towards globalization

What sorts of factors indicate the existence of a process of globalization? Trends towards globalization can be broken down into economic, political, technological and cultural processes, though these are interconnected in reality. First, developments in information technology have meant that it is now a straightforward matter for individuals to communicate instantaneously around the globe. Complex computer information networks enhance the autonomy of the communicators and vastly increase the quantity and complexity of the information that can be exchanged. These developments have occurred against the backdrop of the speed and frequency of international trade and travel contacts in recent decades. Developments in satellite and cable technology have led to the organizing of the electronic media on a global scale. Increasingly, television news is not confined to a single nation or region. Vast distances are effectively shrunk by new technologies; faraway events take on a more immediate character and importance. In this sense we all live in the 'global village'.

Modern technology is transforming the character of global finance and economics. Domestic economic success now largely means success in a highly competitive, knowledge and technology-driven international market. Increasingly, it is argued, the world's largest and most significant transnational corporations (TNCs) are 'stateless', not rooted in one nation or market. They have massive resources: the five largest companies in the world (General Motors, Wal-Mart,

Exxon Mobil, Ford, and Daimler Chrysler) each has revenues higher than the gross domestic product (GDP) of Norway or Singapore, for example, and the annual revenue of General Motors almost equals the GDP of eight countries combined (in this example, Ireland, New Zealand, Uruguay, Sri Lanka, Kenya, Namibia, Nicaragua and Chad) (Hertz 2001). They possess the technological and financial resources to forge a global division of labour, for example by strategic use of less stringent environmental regulations and cheaper labour for production in less developed countries. Many of them are able to treat the whole globe as a single marketplace, freeing themselves to an extent from legal and other constraints arising from national or regional political frameworks. Can such TNCs be held democratically accountable for the impacts upon diverse peoples of their investment and production strategies?

Further, recent decades have witnessed an extraordinary expansion in the numbers, roles and capacities of global *political* and *economic* institutions, some more or less technical in character, such as the International Atomic Energy Authority or the World Meterological Association, others more explicitly political, representing an intensification of decision-making above the level of the nation-state. The United Nations, the World Bank, the International Monetary Fund (IMF), the World Trade Organization and the European Union are the most important (sets of) organizations in an expanding network of authoritative international political actors.

The rise of transnational political issues

Such institutional structures reflect the increasing importance of transnational political issues. By their existence, they also *reinforce* the view that these issues matter a great deal. Prime examples of transnational issues are global warming, the depletion of the earth's protective ozone layer, migration and refugees, the drugs trade, terrorism, the AIDS epidemic, the global gulf between rich and poor, and the trade in arms (many of these are linked to each other). These have joined narrower economic issues, such as investment decisions and currency values, as questions and problems the very nature of which demands effective international organization and mediation. The increasing salience of such global policy problems is paralleled by the increasing visibility of systems designed or adapted to cope with them. The 'Earth Summit' (the United Nations Conference on Environment and Development, or UNCED), held in Rio de Janeiro in 1992, brought together leaders of all countries to negotiate and sign agreements on topics as diverse as global warming, biodiversity, deforestation, and the future character and pace of changes towards sustainability. This was followed up by further agreements in Johannesburg in 2002. The United Nations Conference on Population and Development, held in Cairo in 1994, hammered out an agreement on measures designed to curtail global population growth. The Climate Change Convention held in Kyoto in 1999 reached agreement – which has since threatened to unravel, in particular with the election in 2000 of the environmental sceptic and friend of the oil lobby, George W. Bush, as US president – on measures designed to address the threat of global warming.

Finally, we have witnessed in recent decades the increasing influence and activity of cross-national social movements, operating on the assumption that there are norms and processes which reach automatically beyond the scope of the nation-state. Organizations which pursue environmental objectives, such as Friends of the Earth and Greenpeace, and human rights advocates, such as Amnesty International, are among the most prominent of such actors.

Globalization and national states

There appear to be strong grounds for arguing that national sovereignty or autonomy – the ability of individual states, democratic or not, to determine their own affairs – is being eroded in the face of globalization. But these trends are far from uniform. Clearly different countries, and different regions, experience and perceive globalization in different ways. The impact of globalization on national sovereignty, for example, varies greatly from the richer Northern countries to the developing countries.

David Held has put forward the organizing idea of what he calls 'disjunctures' between the formal authority of the nation-state and the realities of the emerging global system (Held 1991; 1995). Let's look at these briefly, as they help to clarify the ways in which the 'sovereignty' of the nation-state has been under genuine threat. First, Held identifies a disjuncture between 'the formal authority of the state and the actual system of production, distribution and exchange which in many ways serves to limit the power or scope of national political authorities' (Held 1991, 214). Transnational corporations erode state autonomy in that their activities are increasingly organized on a global scale, a key element in the internationalization of production and of financial transactions in the world's major stock markets. National boundaries are no longer so significant as boundaries of economic activity; it is no longer accurate to speak in terms of national markets, given the porous boundaries between the national and the international. The growth and dynamism of the international economy constrains domestic political capacity for economic control and manipulation, a development allied with the emergence of sound economic management as the primary ingredient of sound political management within virtually all states, rich and poor alike. While these trends are far from uniform across the globe, and in places regional organization does afford new forms of national government leverage over economic development (such as the European Union), they do add up to a significant erosion of state autonomy.

Second, Held identifies a major disjuncture in 'the vast array of international regimes and organizations that have been established to manage whole areas of transnational activity . . . and collective policy problems' (Held 1991, 216). To varying degrees, and in different policy areas, the World Bank and the United Nations, for example, now act as more than just a clearing house for multinational decision-making, but have developed policy autonomy. Autonomy for many states in developing countries is severely curtailed under IMF pressures to institute economic and social policies which conform to a common pattern of promoting economic efficiency through 'free' or 'liberalized' markets. The European Union represents a clear case of a shift of autonomy and sovereignty from national states to a set of supra-state institutions – in this case, institutions that resemble those of national governments, with an elected parliament and approximate equivalents to national executives and judicial institutions (see the comments on Lijphart's framework in chapter 2). In the areas of trade and currency especially, the EU already has powers that one would expect a federal *state* to have.

The third disjuncture is the impact on national sovereignty of the development of international law (Held 1991, 218–20). This challenges the traditional autonomy of action within the international arena afforded to states in the pursuit of their own interests. Machinery now exists for the collective enforcement of international rights, most notably perhaps under the European Convention for the Protection of Human Rights and Fundamental Freedoms. Member states of the European Union have successfully been prosecuted for violating basic rights of their citizens under European law. The United Nations Universal Declaration of Human Rights has a more symbolic character, but it too has grown in prominence. Recently, the International War Crimes Tribunal in the Netherlands has broken new ground by achieving the extradition and trial of the war crimes suspect and former Yugoslav president Slobodan Milosevic.

Finally, Held identifies a disjuncture between the idea of the sovereign state and the existence of hegemonic powers and regional power blocs (1991, 220–2). The USA remains the most powerful state in the world, economically, militarily and culturally. The difficulties of making advances in global decision-making without the agreement of the US government have been underlined by President George W. Bush's withdrawal from the Kyoto agreement on global warming, his non-attendance at the World Summit on Sustainable Development in Johannesburg in 2002, and his pursuit of so-called national missile defence in place of certain existing arms treaties. The North Atlantic Treaty Organization (NATO) is arguably becoming an even more vital factor after the Cold War than during it, as its tentacles reach towards some of the states that were former members of the Warsaw Pact, and it actively intervenes in conflicts such as the Bosnian war in the 1990s. The events of September 11, 2001, have reinforced many of these developments.

Different commentators see developments moving in different ways, and predictions vary as to the future of the nation-state. The former European Union science and technology forecaster Riccardo Petrella, for example, has predicted that, 'by the middle of the next century, such nation-states as Germany, Italy, the United States or Japan will no longer be the most relevant socio-economic entities and the ultimate political configuration. Instead, areas like Orange County, California; Osaka, Japan; the Lyon region of France, or Germany's Ruhrgebiete will acquire predominant socio-economic status. The real decision-making powers of the future . . . will be transnational companies in alliance with city-regional governments' (quoted in Toffler and Toffler 1993). Cerny (1999) sees 'the most likely scenario' as a 'durable disorder' he calls 'neomedievalism', in which states are just one element competing with (for example) companies and international networks of organizations in a competitive, fragmented, and essentially undemocratic global 'order'. However possible futures are characterized, many would agree with Dahl that 'the boundaries of a country . . . are now much smaller than the boundaries of the decisions that significantly affect the fundamental interests of its citizens . . . The governments of countries are becoming local governments' (1989, 319).

The impact of globalization on democracy

Focusing more tightly, what has been, and what might be, the impact of globalization upon democracy? In a world where the sovereignty and the autonomy of the nation-state face no significant threats, the notion of democracy as *consent* of the governed has quite a clear meaning and application: each government requires the consent of the citizens who live *within the accepted borders* of the country in question. However, where globalization places into question key aspects of state sovereignty and autonomy, the questions of *whose* consent is democratically required for which actions becomes much more problematic. Should recipients of international aid be able to consent to – or to withdraw their consent for – the particular aid policies of donor governments? Should citizens of other countries which are the unwilling recipients of acid rain from industrial activities have the democratic right, or at least the opportunity, to consent to policies which prolong or worsen those activities? Do democratic principles demand that the increasing influence of footloose transnational corporations on national economic performance be reflected in the establishment of mechanisms for affected citizens of *different* states to have some say in their siting and investment decisions?

Further, has globalization stripped the democratic state of capacities to deliver on promises and programmes that form the very stuff of electoral politics? Does national democracy now result in efforts by competing parties to out-promise each other, while all the while the chances of any of them being able to deliver are slipping away, precisely because of the shifts in economic and political power that we have traced above? In the early twenty-first century, there is a remarked global trend towards citizen distrust of their political leaders and widespread cynicism about political institutions in all liberal democracies. Indeed, one commentator has claimed that 'people have lost faith in politics, because they no longer know what governments are good for. Thanks to the steady withdrawal of the state over the past 20 years from the public sphere, it is corporations, not governments, that increasingly define the public realm' (Hertz 2001, 22).

Normally, each democratic system is assumed to belong within a definite 'political unit', a slice of territory over which it has final authority. We saw in the preceding three chapters just how common this basic assumption has been in thinking about democracy. Dominant Schumpeterian approaches have assumed the existence of the nation-state as *the* political unit for democracy, and their critics have largely followed suit. The unexamined character of the political unit in these narratives has meant that, until quite recently, the question 'who is "the people" if democracy means that the people rule?' has had a pretty definite answer. In the context of globalization, though, we need to ask with a new urgency: what is the appropriate group or community or unit to whom democratic rules apply? If the answer is no longer unambiguously the nation-state, is it the locality? The region? The world? The clients of powerful companies? All of these, depending on what the issue is?

A more immediate and practical problem, perhaps, is the lack of democracy in existing global political institutions. Observers of the European Union are familiar with the problem of the 'democratic deficit' at the heart of the union's institutional structure. The phrase commonly refers to the lack of authority within the union accorded to the only democratically elected body within it, the European Parliament. The United Nations suffers a democratic deficit in particular due to the power of the largely self-selected Security Council, in whose hands lie many of the most crucial decisions about war and peace that are taken under the UN's aegis. The World Bank, the WTO and the IMF have been subjected to criticism about the allegedly largely unaccountable manner in which they operate. Can these key international institutions be put on a more explicitly democratic basis, even if we have to rethink democracy beyond the confines of the nation-state to be able to answer the question?

These, then, are some of the challenges that globalization poses to democracy – its practice, and, prior to that, the very idea of what it is. Core aspects of globalization challenge directly the limitations of the dominant narratives charted in chapters 2 and 3.

Complexity and its consequences

When we look at a range of modern and classical narratives of democracy, such as those covered in chapters 2 and 3, we could be forgiven for thinking that key institutional features of a democratic system are more or less clear and transparent. Certainly, there are large swathes of democratic theory which simplify the world quite drastically. This is understandable; we all need to use simplifying models to describe the world. But one of the key challenges to democracy today lies precisely in the sheer *complexity* of modern government and governance. For example, can citizens participate meaningfully in decision-making processes in which scientific and technical dimensions have become increasingly prominent (such as genetic modification in food production, or cloning, or reproductive technology)? And, are modern democratic government structures now so large and fragmented that they are effectively 'out of control'?

The nature of, and some of the factors behind, this complexity were evident in the discussion of globalization, above. My aim now is to look more broadly and systemically at the impact of complexity, by setting out briefly the types of complexity, the main responses to it by political scientists and by political leaders, and the implications for how democracy might be understood and practised in the light of these responses.

The 'state' is that set of institutions which rules a country. More technically, it claims a monopoly on the legitimate use of violence within a given territory.[2] Often the term 'government' is used to mean the same thing, but using 'state' emphasizes that all 'public' bodies (i.e., those that are not private companies or charities or voluntary associations) are included, however remote they may be (or seem to be) from the heart of a political system.

Types of state complexity

State complexity has four key dimensions. First, *structural* complexity can be seen most clearly in the sheer number and range of organizations that make up the burgeoning executive branches of modern states in particular. The executive in the USA and in the major European democracies, for example, consists of hundreds if not thousands of separate organizations – a bewildering variety of executive departments, bureaus and agencies that perform an array of regulatory, judicial, implementation and advisory roles.

Closely related is *functional* complexity. The functions of governments in the nineteenth, and into the twentieth, century were fairly few and basic – defence, diplomacy, and providing and defending a basic framework of laws. With the development and expansion of the welfare state after World War II, and with efforts by governments to harness scientific and technological progress (nuclear energy for civil purposes, for example), the roles taken on (and created) by the state have changed greatly in both number and type. Further, the publics in modern democracies by and large expect states to take primary responsibility for all key issues that impinge upon the quality of life – health, education, the environment, the workplace, and so on.

Third, *technical* complexity resides in the highly specialized and elusive character of many of the ingredients of a range of policy problems. Increasingly technical complexity makes specialized bodies of experts ever more critical to a full understanding of specific policy options. And the final key dimension of state complexity is the *boundary problem*. Where does the state end and the private sphere begin? It is commonly argued that the boundaries between the public and the private have become blurred. Private organizations, such as corporations, trade unions and professional associations, and charities, often perform public functions (such as welfare functions); at the same time, it is not unusual for public organizations to charge for their services and compete with the private sector in some way.

The implications of state complexity

The implications of complexity for the state and democracy are considerable. The effective sidelining of elected legislatures in some modern democracies is just the first of them. The rapid expansion in state bodies and functions has taken place in the executive branches of modern states; the capacities of legislatures to oversee in any detail, and therefore to offer effective scrutiny of, the work of this greatly expanded executive are limited (though the nature of the political system makes a difference here – see comments on 'majoritarian' versus 'consensus' models in chapter 2). Second, government ministers and heads of large central-government departments or bureaus often have little possibility of understanding, let alone controlling, the vast and fragmented executive structures of which they are the nominal heads. Third, as the technical content of policy has grown, the chances for effective participation by ordinary people in policy-making have diminished. Fourth, there is a danger of what has been called 'ungovernability'. This was a vogue term in the 1970s, as modern Western states found themselves apparently unable to escape a vicious circle of sluggish economic performance, institutional sclerosis and apparently ineffective government. If the state itself cannot be governed, how can it operate as the government of society at large? In various ways, the complexity of the tasks that governments have faced, allied with the complexity of the array of institutions established for the management and resolution of policy problems, may stand as an obstacle to effective decision-making in democracies.

Political scientists have attempted to devise new models of the policy process in order to understand the faces of complexity. Comparatively optimistic and simple models of the transmission of popular opinion to decision-makers in a linear manner dating from the 1950s took on a darker tone in the wake of stagflation, institutional sclerosis, economic downturn, Vietnam and Watergate (for example). These new models sometimes challenged Schumpeterian assumptions. Robert Dahl, whose model of 'polyarchy' was canvassed in chapter 2, was suggesting by 1989 that there was a 'polyarchy II' in which 'the mobilization of specialized intelligence in the service of modern government' was designed to meet the needs of expanding governments with expanding policy range and scope. But giving experts primary governing roles in conjunction with the people's representatives carried dangers for democracy, making it more like 'guardianship' – Dahl's term for democracy's major opponent. Dahl feared that modern democratic systems were moving to a position where policy was becoming so complex that 'We could no longer properly interpret Polyarchy II as a grafting of the expertness of guardianship to the popular sovereignty of the demos. We might have to interpret it instead as the grafting of the symbols of democracy to the de facto guardianship of the policy elites' (Dahl 1989, 337).

The network metaphor

The most prominent metaphor to express the non-linear, non-hierarchical, fragmented character of politics and policy in the complex state, prominent in writing from Western Europe and the USA, has been that of the 'policy network'. Policy networks were groupings of state and private organizations

and individuals which often housed the real locus of negoti-
ated power over policy in a number of domains (agriculture
and health were two well-documented areas in studies on
both sides of the Atlantic). They reflected a 'post-parliamen-
tary' democracy in the UK, and the importance of relatively
hidden 'sub-system' politics in the USA. They came about
as a result of various trends linked directly to complexity:
specialization and fragmentation in policy-making, greater
mobilization of competing interests, the wider scope of state
functions, growth in the size of the state structure, and
increasingly blurred boundaries between public and private.
Networks helped, in theory at least, to channel and restrict
access to decision-making, regularize policy consultation and
negotiation, supply a means of coordination in the absence
of effective, traditional linear hierarchies, and not least to
help to implement policy.

How might democracy adapt to cope with state complexity and network governance? Two of the new innovations
in the idea of democracy to be considered in the following chapter resonate with the concerns about complexity
and accountability: the *deliberative* and the *associative*
approaches to democracy. The former, a version of which is
briefly touted by Dahl using the tag 'polyarchy III', suggests
that new deliberative forums can render complex issues and
processes newly accessible to ordinary citizens. The idea of
associative democracy, on the other hand, envisions a radical
devolution of policy and service-delivery to essentially private
associations outside the state itself – a way of giving politics
back to the people, after a fashion. Each of these will be discussed in detail below.

The environment and future generations

Familiar accounts of our world, especially the ones that shape
the circumstances of our daily lives, seem to us to offer a complete account of their subjects. The dominant narrative of
democracy charted in chapter 2 seemed for so long to represent the very span of democracy's possibilities, in the West
at least. Sometimes it takes a surprisingly new and fresh

perspective to show up the hitherto unimagined shortcomings of familiar narratives – their blind spots, no-go areas, and reliance on received wisdom. Feminist criticism had this impact on the dominant Schumpeterian narrative, for example, highlighting the ways in which the latter's public–private distinction masked fundamental gender inequalities. The rapid emergence and political impact of environmentalism brought something similar, a new 'angle' which revealed key limitations of conventional ideas about democracy.

A spectrum of 'green' views

The impact of environmentalism on the practice and the theory of democracy can best be explored in terms of the spectrum of views which environmentalism contains; the electoral and policy impact of green parties and pressure groups in a number of Western democracies; and the relationship between the respective ideals of democracy and environmentalism. Each of these areas helps us in turn to pinpoint the challenges environmentalism poses for democracy.

Environmentalism encompasses many different shades of opinion. Nevertheless, some core environmentalist values can be identified. According to the near-canonical *Programme of the German Green Party* (1983), environmentalism's four basic principles are: (a) the ecological, based on the perceived need for political and economic systems which protect the stability of ecosystems; (b) the social, underlining commitments to social justice, self-determination and the quality of life; (c) grassroots democracy, incorporating calls for decentralization and direct democracy; and (d) non-violence, derived from the notion that 'human goals cannot be achieved by inhumane means'. Further, globalism (rather than nationalism or isolationism) and a concern about the long-term impact of past and present actions are often put forward as guiding principles of environmentalism.

In recent years the principle of *sustainability* – sometimes 'sustainable development' – has come to occupy a central place in environmentalist thinking and policy proposals. The influential report in 1987 of the United Nations World

Commission on Environment and Development, *Our Common Future*, defined sustainable development as 'development that meets the needs of the present generation without compromising the ability of future generations to meet their own needs'. Conceptions of environmental sustainability can vary along a number of dimensions – just what is to be sustained (the human-made as well as the natural?), why it should be sustained (human welfare or nature's value too?), and for whom (present humans and non-humans or future ones too?) (Dobson 1996a). Clearly, the concept of sustainability allows of many interpretations, from relatively small adjustments to current economic policies and technological developments to a more radical overhaul of political and economic institutions (see Barry 1999).

A common distinction is made within environmentalism between what is termed 'shallow' and 'deep' ecology, or between 'light' greens and 'dark' greens. Broadly speaking, light greens pursue reform strategies through the existing institutions of Western democracies, while dark greens express a greater distrust of existing forms and institutions of democratic politics, often regarding liberal representative democracy in its current form as being deeply *implicated* in environmental degradation. Could democratic politics be partially to *blame* for the environmental crisis? It is fair to say that non-democratic regimes, such as the former Soviet Union and its East European satellites, tended to have worse environmental records than broadly democratic countries. At the same time, the understandable impulse of democratic leaders to wish to satisfy the desires of would-be voters – be they 'green' desires or not – can militate strongly against environmentally friendly outcomes. Although some environmental writers in the 1970s were suspicious of democracy for this reason, 'greens' today applaud democratic methods, and indeed often press for more radical, grassroots and deliberative forms of democratic practice (see the discussion in the following chapter).

In the case of the greens, like that of others, attitudes to democracy reflect wider commitments and concerns. Greens make different ethical assumptions about humans and their roles within (and relationships to) the natural environment. Human-centred (or 'anthropocentric') approaches to environmentalism stress the conservation and preservation of natural resources because the latter are useful to humans, for example, because they provide a resource for recreation. This approach overlaps with that of the dominant neo-Schumpeterian narrative of democracy, which places humanity at the centre of democracy's universe. More radical, or 'ecocentric' (earth-centred), approaches assert that sentience, life and/or naturally self-renewing processes have value in themselves, quite apart from whatever instrumental value they may have for humans. This alternative view opens up the provocative prospect of political systems which incorporate the interests of non-humans and future generations into formal decision-making procedures, alongside the interest of voters, who (we assume) represent *present generation human* interests. In the next chapter we will see how political ecologists propose that we proceed along this path.

The impact of environmentalism

Within mainstream democratic politics, the electoral and policy impact of environmentalism has been considerable – though many greens would argue that there have been significant reverses too, and a good deal of green tokenism. Springing from rising political concern with such issues as pollution, irreversible resource depletion, overpopulation and opposition to nuclear power in the early 1970s, environmental pressure groups such as Friends of the Earth and Greenpeace have gained high memberships, in a number of West European countries much higher than those of even the major political parties, and a high profile in the day-to-day politics of a number of Western democracies. The internationalist and explicitly ethical outlook of this new wave of interest groups has helped to set them apart from more traditional labour-, business- and profession-based interest groups. Indeed, it is sometimes asserted that a new class, concerned with quality of life issues rather than further material gain, has formed the bedrock of support for environmentalism.

The major electoral breakthrough for green political parties was the election in 1983 of Green Party candidates to the lower house of the (then) West German national parliament, the Bundestag. The 1989 elections to the European Parliament were an electoral high point for green parties, with the previously little-known British and French parties, for example, respectively gaining 14.9 per cent and 10.6 per cent of the national vote. At that time, great media prominence was granted to such problems as the Chernobyl nuclear accident, global warming, acid rain, and the depletion of the earth's protective ozone layer.

The pinnacle in terms of electoral and governmental success was reached in 1998 with the formation of the red–green national coalition government in Germany, which persists at the time of writing, with prominent Green Party ministers including the foreign minister Joshka Fischer. The German Green Party is easily the most prominent of the world's environmentalist parties, and in terms of principles, policy and organization has been a significant influence on green parties in other countries. In other European countries, notably Britain, France, the Netherlands, Belgium and Italy, green parties now have an established place in electoral politics (though their electoral performances have been uneven from the 1980s into the new century, and are highly dependent upon a country's electoral system).

Government action on the environment

In the face of considerable political and scientific pressure, governments in some Western democracies have adopted and, to some degree, acted upon quite comprehensive environmental policy plans, covering such areas as pollution control, health, transport, agriculture and the urban environment. Further, supra-national bodies and summit meetings have played an increasingly crucial role in developing comprehensive environmental policies and treaties – appropriately enough, since problems such as climate change, ozone depletion and access to basic resources in poorer countries cannot by their very nature be addressed effectively by national governments acting alone. Environmental policy has been a core concern of the European Union, especially since the mid-

1980s, and at the United Nations Conference on Environment and Development at Rio de Janeiro in 1992 (the 'Earth Summit') the largest ever gathering of heads of government resulted in agreements of varying strength on climate change, biodiversity, deforestation, aid and sustainable development. Forging international agreements on the environment has been no easy matter, however: the Rio Summit brought to the surface simmering arguments between the rich North and the poorer states of the South over which is the worst environmental offender and who should make the greater economic sacrifice in the name of environmental protection. These debates continued unabated at the World Summit on Sustainable Development held in Johannesburg in August 2002. And, since 2001, the US government's refusal to endorse, or work within the framework of, the Kyoto agreement on combating climate change has resulted in great uncertainty and difficulty regarding how fossil-fuel emissions might be tackled in an effective way (the USA being the single biggest international offender in the relevant regards).

A radical green democracy?

The most distinctive *visions* of green democracy have been quite utopian variants on the theme of direct democracy in a small and often rural community, characterized by self-reliance and labour-intensive production. One influential account of this model is 'bioregionalism', which holds that human communities should be organized according to features of the natural world – clearly a doctrine which would have major implications for the future of democracy and the nation-state as we know it (Sale 1985). These direct democratic and decentralist ideals have found *some* practical expression in the organization of green parties, notably in the earlier years of the German Green Party, where, for example, the basic principle of 'grassroots democracy' was translated into the wide local participation in the formulation of policy and the rotation of parliamentary leaders (with an eye to preventing the emergence of an elite leadership). However, such radical visions can create logical problems. For example, if instituting direct democracy means that public policies will more closely reflect the wishes of citizens, then a direct democrat must surely feel constrained by the expression of the popular will through (for example) elections and referendums. What if the citizenry do not *want* green outcomes? In such a case, presumably something has to give – either the environmentalist goals of (for instance) lower consumption and uses of alternative sources of energy must be diluted or abandoned, according to the popular will, or the commitment to (direct) democracy must itself be softened. Or, alternatively, 'democracy' itself has to be rethought quite fundamentally – perhaps on a traditional view (like Schumpeterian ones) it has been biased towards human needs and interests and away from those of non-human animals and entities? Perhaps, too, democracy as we know it is biased towards the interests of present generations of humans and against the interests of future generations? Could what we think of as 'democracy' possibly adapt to encompass the concerns behind such radical questioning?

Each of these possibilities bears on the most pressing political challenge, namely how to find ways in which a world of competing nation-states might be encouraged to act in principled concert. We will look at some thought-provoking ideas on how some of the challenges might be met by rethinking democracy, in the next chapter.

The challenge of versatility

Can democracy take root and thrive in different cultural and religious soils, or is it 'culturally particular', relevant only to 'the West'? Like the others discussed in this chapter, this question represents an enormous topic in its own right. I confine myself to making a couple of points in outline, to the effect that, although democracy has universal value (at least in the sense that sizeable numbers of people in very different cultures *do* value it), we must expect that it will mean and be different things in different cultures and contexts, and not that it will be a copy of a conventional Western liberal model everywhere.

All democrats now?

Political science interest in transitions from non-democratic government to democracy, and in the conditions for the consolidation of democracy in newly democratized countries, has been great in recent years, especially in the light of the Eastern European revolutions of 1989. These tumultuous recent events renewed what has been called the 'third wave' of democratization (Huntington 1991). The first wave was from the mid-nineteenth century up to the 1920s, and the second in the years following World War II. The current third wave began in the mid-1970s in Portugal and Spain, and continues (haltingly) in Africa and Latin America, for example. No transition to democracy is ever straightforward or entirely predictable. Much ink has been spilled debating the conditions that may or may not assist in the process of attempting to consolidate democracy in newly democratizing countries. In the end, much seems to depend on circumstances of individual countries (Lewis 1997). Insofar as factors can be pinpointed that may aid consolidation, they have included the state of economic development, the nature of class and social divisions, which institutions are established, and the character of the initial transition (Beetham 1999, 67–86).

Despite the great challenges facing democracy, for the first time in history more than half of the world's countries are governed by leaders who can make some plausible claim to democratic legitimacy. That, at least, is the wider, global picture. However, such a broad picture does not necessarily tell us a great deal about democracy's relevance and versatility across cultural and other contexts. We would need much more local, fine-grained analyses to see beyond simple models of national *electoral* democracy in order to, for example, gauge the actual nature of the reception and understanding of democracy in its contexts. The fact remains that the 'stable democracies' of the world are concentrated in the rich Northern countries with broadly liberal cultures and capitalist economies, and which were colonial powers in the past. There are very significant variations here – the largest democracy in the world, by far, for example, is an ex-colony and a developing country (India), and in Africa and Latin America in recent decades the advance of electoral democracy has been significant if sometimes fragile. But a key question, and challenge, remains: can Western, liberal models of democracy adapt to quite different cultural contexts?

Cultural values and democracy

Within waves of democracy, one key issue that is easily overlooked in the global scheme of things is the relationship between democracy and local cultures, religions and practices. It is all too easy to assume that democracy is a one-size-fits-all affair. It is clear enough that in *any* given system there will be much dispute about how cultural traditions and histories ought to be understood, and the extent to which they should qualify or constrain democratic structures and practices. There may even be a case for saying that there can be perfectly legitimate non-democracies; one could suggest, for example, that Tibet before the completion of Chinese occupation in 1959 might be a clear – and rare – example, where elite rule on the basis of perceived superior knowledge was almost universally accepted. Often, Western critics assume that (a) democracy is Western and (b) democracy is not compatible with many aspects of non-Western cultures. The Islamic religion is often a target in this respect.

Often, too, the defence of democracy comes most robustly from those who supposedly ought to reject it because of their opposing values. Even in this case of Tibet, the (Chinese-occupied) country's political and spiritual leader, the Dalai Lama, has written recently of 'the need for firm conviction on all our parts in acknowledging the universality of the key ethical and political values that underlie democracy' (1999, 3). Relatedly, the popular dissident leader of Buddhist Burma, Aung San Suu Kyi, has suggested that: 'It is a strong argument for democracy that governments regulated by principles of accountability, respect for public opinion and the supremacy of just laws are more likely than an all-powerful ruler or ruling class, uninhibited by the need to honour the will of the people, to observe the traditional duties of Buddhist kingship. Traditional values serve both to justify and to decipher popular expectations of democratic government' (1991, 173).

Islam and democracy

There is a great deal of argument in many Muslim countries, among political figures as much as among scholars, on the vexed issue of the compatibility of Islam with democracy. The events of September 11, 2001, reinvigorated this debate, though it has not always been well informed about either Islam or democracy. One route into this question, pursued by the Iranian scholar Hamid Enayat, notes that, 'If Islam comes into conflict with certain postulates of democracy, it is because of its *general* character as a religion' (1982, 126) – 'all efforts to synthesize Islam and democracy are bound to founder on the bedrock of that body of eternal and unchangeable doctrines which form the quintessence of every religion' (1982, 135). At the same time, he is keen to point out 'theoretical affinities' between democracy and Islam: Islam has strong concepts of equality, the rule of law, and taking on board the wishes of the ruled in the making of collective decisions, through principles of 'shura' (consultation) and 'ijma' (consensus) (1982, 127–9).

Political Islam has gained enormously in strength in recent years across the Arab world and beyond. The 'Islamism' propounded by groups such as Hizbullah in Lebanon, Hamas in the Palestinian Occupied Territories, or the FIS and GIA in Algeria is no monolithic set of beliefs or practices. Some of these movements have at times spoken of hostility to 'democracy', though that can mean hostility to 'the West', for example, as much as to any particular political institutions. At best, the sort of approach taken by Enayat could establish some areas of general compatibility between 'Islam' and 'democracy'. But here we need to exercise great care. The comparison cannot be conducted in wholly *Western* terms, not least since 'The principle of the functionality of the Islamist discourse is . . . to make at least a symbolic rupture with the universe of Western culture' (Burgat and Dowell 1993, 121). The comparison arguably needs to be conducted on the basis of the values and the 'essential nature' of Islamism, keeping in mind all the while that no cultural or political system, including a religious-dominated one, is by any means impervious to significant change or internal disputes over essential meanings. In other words, there is a case for saying that on such issues we need to shift away from a Western centre of gravity in our thinking about the meaning and the demands of democracy. Certainly there are examples of trenchant Islamist opposition to democracy. At the same time, with leading Islamist intellectuals such as Rachid Ghannouchi (Tunisia) and Abdul Karim Soroush (Iran), there is a trend for Islamist thinkers to 'surmount' the anti-democratic 'reactionary phase' of Islamism in order to embrace, in one way or another, values of 'democratic pluralism' (Burgat and Dowell 1993, 127). Interestingly, this sometimes seems to point to the *inherency*, and not the more static *compatibility*, of basic democratic principles in Islam. Key thinkers seem to oscillate between these two views; compare the words of Soroush and Ghannouchi: '[For Soroush], at the top of the list is democracy. Although Islam literally means "submission", Soroush argues that there is no contradiction between Islam and the freedoms inherent in democracy. "Islam and democracy are not only compatible, their association is inevitable"' (Wright 1996, 68); Ghannouchi comments that: 'Decision making, through the process of shura, belongs to the community as a whole. Thus the democratic values of political pluralism and tolerance are perfectly compatible with Islam' (Wright 1996, 72). In the case of Iran, at least, Soroush's ideas have had a significant impact within debates about the country's becoming an established Islamic democracy or republic.

Democracy travels

We have to be sensitive also in these debates to the slipperiness of language itself. Schaffer (1998) records how the word 'demokaraasi' for Wolof speakers in Senegal takes on particular meaning and significance within the distinctive Senegalese context. He writes, for example,

> Non-francophone Wolof speakers . . . have adapted this word to their own culture and conditions. For them *demokaraasi* has continued to be associated with elections, voting, and multipartyism, associations that correspond most closely to those of its French progenitor. The word has, however, taken

on added meanings of consensus, solidarity, and evenhanded-
ness, meanings derived in part from the Wolof discourse of
the political elite and in part from an ethic of mutuality rooted
in a pervasive condition of economic precariousness.
(Schaffer 1998, 80)

It is a question not just of dilutions or adaptions of standard
democratic institutions, but of the very altered meanings as
democracy and related terms are translated between radically
differing cultural contexts.

It seems that cultural sensitivity is a real challenge to
our ideas of democracy. There are no wholly non-Western
models of democracy, of course, because modernity is
Western and it impinges everywhere. But there can be significant, and legitimate, adaptions, variations and institutional innovations of democratic understanding and practice,
as thinkers and practitioners in non-Western societies chart
their ways on new democratic 'paths in the global village'
(Dallmayr 1998).

Surprising affinities?

One final, speculative, comment: often, the target of non-
Western critics is liberalism, or permissive, often self-seeking,
individualism; 'Western democracy' comes under fire (by proponents of 'Asian values', by some Islamists, by comparison
with indigenous 'democratic' cultures, by proponents of
African one-party or no-party 'democracies') by virtue of its
intimate and inevitable association with liberal individualism.
It is worth noting that the dominant thread in recent *Anglo-
American* democratic theory has had a roughly similar character. Republicanism and communitarianism have undergone
major revivals, with renewed stress on ideas such as the
importance of deliberation aimed at achieving the common
good in an expanded public space in which all are prepared
to take on common responsibilities. Perhaps there is more
than merely rhetorical overlap with, for example, alleged
African traditions of face-to-face community consensus-
seeking, and the general idea that unanimity, consensus and
talk are at the heart of a proper democracy. It would be a
mistake to overdraw these links, but if 'insofar as liberalism

tends toward instability and dissociation, it requires periodic communitarian correction' (Walzer 1990, 21), then it may come as no surprise that similar discourses of common responsibility and obligation may at certain times find resonance in Western and non-Western contexts. Certainly there appears to be a striking commonality of values between key elements of contemporary Anglo-American and – in particular – the traditional African discourse (and, if Manglapus (1987) is right, many indigenous 'original democracies' on many continents).

Democracy must be adapted to context in order to take root in that context. It will have to be *Islamic* democracy, or *Chinese* or *Senegalese* democracy.[3] Just what *these* prefixes mean will no doubt remain highly contestable. But the key point is that, if democracy is to continue to spread, it will need to continue to adapt to diverse cultural contexts. Rapidly increasing percentages of the world's population live in developing countries outside 'the West'. In this light, one might argue that the serial 'indigenization' of democracy represents its future. Perhaps, if there is a 'fourth wave' of democratization, it is about stretching and moulding the depth and character of democracy, rather than simply its geographical spread.

Conclusion

Democracy does not always thrive, but when it does it is only because it meets challenges that pose fundamental questions about its meaning and value. In the following chapter, we will consider a range of new, innovative ideas about how democracy might be reconstructed to meet a range of pressing challenges, not least those outlined above. While no watertight symmetry exists between the challenges to democracy and the new approaches discussed in the next chapter (nothing about democratic politics is ever that straightforward), broadly speaking we can say that: innovative deliberative and ecological ideas can be used to address the environmentalist challenge; cosmopolitan and deliberative models provide resources for thinking about globalization; deliberative and associative models provide potential responses to the challenges of complexity; and ideas of deliberation and 'difference' democracy do likewise for some of the challenges of versatility.

5
Reinventing Democracy

One of the ironies of politics in the early twenty-first century is that widespread apathy about electoral and representative democracy is accompanied by creative and original thinking about how democracy might be reinvented to meet the types of major challenge outlined in chapter 4. In this final chapter we explore possible democratic futures by scanning a selection of today's most discussed democratic innovations – *deliberative, direct, cosmopolitan, ecological, 'politics of presence', associative and party-based models*. These models are not entirely new, of course; they build upon earlier narratives of democracy by adding new twists to familiar plotlines. Indeed, these innovative models can best be understood if we focus on exactly where and how they depart from the familiar narratives. This is the approach I adopt.

The scope of the analysis is broad, but it is also restricted in the following ways: the six innovative ideas scrutinized arise from, and largely (though not exclusively) address, countries of the rich North rather than the developing South; they do not exhaust the range of current innovations in democratic theory; and they are based largely in English-language sources.

Six dimensions of democracy

When we look at ideas that are put forward as new or innovative, we have to ask 'new or innovative with respect to *what?*' So before we turn to the new ideas, let's establish a kind of baseline against which we might assess some of their features. I suggest that there are six key *dimensions* of democracy. A model or theory of democracy will have something to say on most of these dimensions, making the latter a useful tool for comparing different models, etc. The dimensions are expressed below in the form of questions. For ease of reference, they are designated 'A–F', below and subsequently. To help fix our bearings, I offer brief illustrative comments for each question or dimension, showing how the main narratives of democracy which we examined in earlier chapters might respond in terms of these categories.

Dimension A – space and belonging

How ought the political unit and political community in which democracy is to be practised be understood, in terms of geography, population size, terms of membership (or citizenship) and degree of cultural homogeneity?

Both Schumpeterian and participative narratives unquestioningly regarded the nation-state as the basic political unit for democracy. Participationists went further, emphasizing the importance of smaller 'political units' within nations, such as the workplace. In both narratives culture was rarely mentioned, with the implicit assumption being one of national cultural homogeneity. Marxists and feminists, on the other hand, have stressed solidarity of working classes and women across geographical borders.

Dimension B – rights

What constitutional constraints should democratic majorities face, if any? What rights, if any, should be guaranteed to members or citizens of a democracy?

Schumpeter himself stressed citizen obligations rather than rights, though later accounts (such as Dahl's and Lijphart's) redressed this balance somewhat. Participative theorists stressed participative rights. Neither narrative highlighted the importance of limiting national majorities, particularly. Marxists looked beyond the issue of rights, seeing them as tokenistic, towards a more substantial right to the fruits of one's labour. Feminists have emphasized the ways in which liberal rights have constituted an image of the individual which is that of the independent *man*, ignoring the gendered nature of these seemingly neutral concepts and categories.

Dimension C – group autonomy

To what degree and over what concerns should distinct sub-groups, functional or territorial, possess rights to autonomy or collective self-determination?

Post-Schumpeterian narratives came to take territorial decentralization seriously, especially in Lijphart's work; participationists were keenly concerned with the need for a degree of functional group autonomy in order to empower people where they worked in particular. Marxists always took a broader view, stressing how class groups were the most basic in society, and that the working class possessed interests which in reality dwarfed their division into nations and other territorial or cultural units.

Dimension D – participation

What is to be the balance between different forms of popular participation in the making of collective decisions, in terms of both (a) the balance between direct and representative institutions and (b) the balance of variation within each of these two basic forms?

Schumpeterian narratives do not encompass any need for direct democracy; indeed, the emphasis on quite strictly indirect democracy working through elections and representative institutions was close to being a *defining* feature of such narratives. Even the participationists did not write much about direct democracy, with the partial exception of C. B. MacPherson (1977) and, later, Benjamin Barber (1984), preferring the broader participatory label. Some Marxist traditions have emphasized local and direct forms of democracy and participation, picking up, for example, Marx's own writings on the Paris Commune of 1871.

Dimension E – accountability

How are relations of accountability to be structured, how are 'accounts' to be given, by whom and to whom?

Accountability in these narratives concerned *electoral* accounts. The participatory narrative stretched to accountability within functional groups (such as those working together for one company, or members of a political party). But either way accountability was understood as a formal process centred upon election. For Marxists and feminists, formal modes of 'bourgeois' or 'patriarchal' accountability were limited and tokenistic in the face of fundamental social power imbalances.

Dimension F – public and private

How are the respective roles of the public and the private spheres, and formal and informal modes of political activity, to be understood, and which is taken to provide what in terms of the requirements of a healthy democratic structure?

Schumpeterian narratives confine their concerns about democracy largely to the public sphere, that is the sphere of government and the state. Participationists stretched it outside the state and into civil society in the form of the economic sphere especially. Marxists had long started the other way around, seeing the formal structures of the state as superstructures arising from the real engine-room of society, the economy and the class structure that sprang from it. Feminists later placed this issue at the heart of democracy from another angle, digging further into the 'private' to suggest that 'the personal is political', thus encompassing, for example, the politics of sexuality and the family.

The orthodox line?

To reiterate: these are the dimensions along which different visions of democracy vary. They represent a set of issues on which any self-respecting model or theory of democracy will take a position. Would-be innovative theories may, for example, shift emphases within a dimension; downgrade the importance of any one dimension and highlight the importance of others; or fundamentally reinterpret how a given dimension ought to be understood. We shall see instances of all three strategies with respect to the ideas discussed below.

Of course, responses to these core issues historically have varied enormously. Nevertheless, and with special reference to thinking associated with Schumpeterian narratives, certain lines of liberal democratic orthodoxy – a kind of 'default mode' democracy – are reasonably clear. We can say, without doing too much violence to a complex subject, that the dominant modern narrative of democracy has been characterized by the advocacy or acceptance of primarily *representative* institutions [D]. Allied with this, politics and therefore democracy has been conceived as occurring largely *within the formal structure of the state* [F]. The formal range of the jurisdiction of that state has been defined in terms of national *territorial* units [A] on the basis of *majority rule* [B] constrained largely by guaranteed rights to expressive, associative and basic political freedoms only. Elected and appointed officials exercise considerable policy *discretion* in the context of lines of *formal and hierarchical accountability* [E]. Distinct territorial sub-groups would have tightly *circumscribed autonomy* (if any) from the central state within a specific scope [C].

I put this sketch of orthodoxy forward as a baseline for considering my main focus – the key democratic innovations for the twenty-first century.

New directions for democracy

Full-blown accounts of each of each of these innovations can be found elsewhere (see the references below, and in the

Guide to Further Reading). Here I confine myself to brief indications of how and where the key innovations arise.

Deliberative democracy

The deliberative model of democracy has been the dominant new strand in democratic theory over the past ten to fifteen years. It has had a great impact on how we think about the various dimensions of democracy – perhaps most notably on the question of accountability [E]. This model arose (variously) out of concern that dominant 'aggregative' conceptions of democracy, which focus on voting and elections – essentially, counting heads – were deeply inadequate. Instead, democracy must involve *discussion* on an equal and inclusive basis. This discussion should deepen participant knowledge of issues and awareness of the interests of others, and help to instil the confidence to play an active part in public affairs. Deliberative democracy looks to *transform* people's (possibly ill-informed) preferences through open and inclusive discussion, not merely to design electoral procedures to *reflect* them. It seeks to go beyond the 'mere' design of mechanisms to register the preferences that people already have.

There are markedly different conceptions of deliberative democracy. Theorists and commentators differ, for example, over:

- who should do the deliberating;
- the extent to which certain standards of 'rationality' should govern discussions;
- the collective goal of deliberation (consensus, truth, working agreement?);
- the individual goal (enlightenment, confidence, empowerment?); and
- the appropriate siting of deliberative forums (courts, parliaments, specially designed citizens' forums, political parties, local communities, among the oppressed, in social movements, within the state, against the state, within national boundaries, across national boundaries?).

A reasonable stab at a common definition is that of Bohman: 'Deliberative democracy, broadly defined, is . . . any one of a family of views according to which the public deliberation of free and equal citizens is the core of legitimate political decision making and self-government' (Bohman 1998, 401). Deliberative democracy's impact on our understanding of most of the dimensions of democracy has been significant. Some versions, notably Dryzek's 'discursive democracy', have reinforced the prospect of democracy operating across national and other borders [A]; perhaps across cultural borders as well, laying stress on procedural means by which heterogeneous groups may be able to cooperate through open-ended and inclusive processes built around properly facilitated discussion of agendas and options [C].

The issue of what majorities can do in a democracy, and what rights individuals may have against majorities [B], is given a distinctive spin by the deliberative conception – a spin that is likely to prove influential. Deliberationists generally take the view that constitutional rights cannot be taken for granted as having universal status and applicability, or general justification; they must instead be justified deliberatively themselves, and to that extent they remain *provisional*.[1] At the same time, deliberationists have placed a question mark against the very notion of a 'majority'; there is nothing especially worthy, in democratic terms, they argue, about an aggregate majority of views which simply reflects popular ignorance or prejudice on the issues. If the conventional question has been 'what constitutional constraints should democratic majorities face?', then the new deliberative version suggests replacing 'constitutional' with 'deliberative', and leaving the status of the constraints open to deliberative revision.

In one sense, the deliberative conception downgrades the importance of the direct versus representative debate in democratic theory [D] – each is less than adequate to democratic purposes if it fails to be sufficiently deliberative as well. All adult citizens may have an equal *vote*, but will their *voice* have equal weight in democratic deliberation? Can inclusiveness in this larger sense be achieved? Will the model deliberative forum be like a university seminar, following (sometimes, at any rate) certain canons of rational debate, appropriate evidence and so forth? If so, it may be exclusive because those notions of what counts as rational discourse differ from one group to another. The results may rapidly be overrun by the irrationalities of normal, competitive politics anyhow. Can key deliberative arenas be flexible and inclusive enough to embrace cultural difference in highly pluralistic post-modern societies?

Deliberative conceptions have transformed our view of accountability [E]. Rather than expressing a property of a line-hierarchy – e.g., the civil servant is accountable to the minister, the minister to parliament, parliament to the people – deliberative democracy places renewed stress on accountability as the *ongoing giving of accounts, explanations, or reasons* to those subject to decisions. As such it prompts us to reinterpret such subjects as freedom of information, the accessibility of parliamentary procedure, and the role of broadcasting and the internet in fostering links between representatives and constituencies. Further, it renders much more flexible our notions of who must give accounts to whom (e.g., non-elected officials can be held to various forms of deliberative accountability).

With regard to the sixth dimension [F], deliberative democracy, especially in versions influenced by the work of the prominent German social theorist Jürgen Habermas (1996), has emphasized the importance of a fluid, dynamic process of 'opinion-formation' in the non-state public sphere; some who are influenced by Habermas now seek to go beyond his latest framework to underline even further the greater scope that exists for authentic democratic action outside the constricting formal boundaries of formal state structures – the essence of John Dryzek's (2000) influential 'discursive' model.

In these respects, deliberative conceptions have not so much shifted perspectives within the six dimensions as demanded that we rethink what we *mean* by them. The meanings of belonging, rights, participation and accountability have been profoundly affected by the deliberative current. Important questions remain, however. One especially critical one is: where does or should deliberation occur? The possibilities canvassed in the literature include:

- in specially constructed micro-forums such as 'deliberative opinion polls' and citizens' juries, where a small representative sample of people debate and in some cases vote on issues;

- within political parties;
- in national and other parliaments;
- in supra-national committee networks such as those in the governing structures of the European Union;
- within private or voluntary associations;
- within courts; or
- within a diverse 'public' sphere of 'protected enclaves' or 'subaltern counterpublics',[2] in other words, oppressed groups in society.

Deliberative democrats will continue to be pressed on who is to do the deliberating, and where, and with what links to other decision-making institutions. Continuing practical experiments in the USA, Australia and various West European countries with deliberative opinion polls and citizens' juries provide one sort of response to the 'who' and 'where' questions from within deliberative theory; but there are other ways that offer sometimes radically different responses – not least in the following democratic innovations.

Direct democracy

We turn now to the oldest innovation in democratic thought – direct democracy. The main recent innovation in this area, in terms of its impact on theory and practice, is the 'party-based' model explained and advocated by Budge (1996; 2000). Each of the innovations considered in this chapter has elements which shade into the territory of direct democracy. The local orientation of associative democracy and many ecological visions has a 'direct' quality; deliberative forums too, insofar as ordinary citizens get to participate. The need for cross-border referendums is discussed as part of the cosmopolitan model. Clearly, the categories we are working with are not watertight.

As Budge sees it, the idea of a party-based direct democracy involves 'the people' in effect becoming a third house of a national legislature. Major policy proposals, or bills, passed in the representative legislature would go to a national referendum vote. Propositions would become law only if they passed in a referendum, according to criteria which may include thresholds (or super-majorities) rather than simple majority rule. In this system, political parties would continue to run candidates for elective public offices, form governments, propose legislation, and so forth. In Budge's schema, however, they would in addition campaign for their preferred outcomes in regular policy referendums.

Budge is keen to avoid the problems of what he calls 'unmediated' direct democracy – easily dismissed as utopian or unworkable by direct democracy's critics – in which representative or secondary institutions such as parliaments, parties and even governments are assumed not to be necessary, or have no role. Any serious vision of direct democracy today must see it as operating alongside, or more clearly as part of, a larger democratic system which includes (for example) elected parliaments and political parties. It is here that we can see the major contribution to democratic reconstruction of this model – the effective collapsing of any simple and strong distinction between direct and representative democracy, and within that the assertion of new, practical conceptions of direct democracy which challenge the widespread perception that it is unworkable in modern conditions.

In the party-based vision, direct forms of policy accountability via the referendum (dimension [E]) become much more feasible and desirable since people are now much more educated, and can make sensible choices on policies (especially if still guided by parties). Developments in technology facilitate debate and decision-making capacity for citizens, though there is no easy or obvious route to 'teledemocracy' (Arterton 1987). The suggestion is that higher levels of citizen education, along with widespread access to and capacity to use relevant information, both justify and make practical the view that important government proposals should be put to the people in referendums before becoming law.

One could conjecture that the direct–representative distinction will indeed be, and come to be seen to be, less important in advanced states in the future. This in part reflects the fact that direct democracy requires indirect (representative, administrative, facilitative) institutions for its realistic functioning, such that pressures to increase the scope for direct decision-making will reinforce appropriate indirect structures. One might add that the emphasis on talk, discussion and deliberation will likely continue to downgrade the significance of hard-and-fast representative–direct distinctions – though the importance of voting and elections generally will remain.

Direct democracy in the form of the referendum comes in a range of types. If the referendum is desirable in principle, then some basic choices must be made about how it might be deployed. First of all, should it be:

- conducted nationally, regionally or locally, depending on the issue?
- controlled by government, or the product of citizen initiatives (petitions) or some form of independent commission?
- confined to use on constitutional questions (basic rules of the system, such as who has voting rights), or extended to cover some legislative questions (everyday laws) as well?
- binding on governments, so that they must enact the outcome, or merely consultative, so that they can ignore the outcome if they wish (or maybe both, depending on the issue)?
- one vote decides the issue, or renewable so as to reflect changing citizen attitudes?

In addition, other specific questions about the context in which referendums are held will invariably arise, such as: how should the question be framed? How can more or less equal publicity for all sides be achieved? And what is the appropriate timing?

There are many objections to using any forms of direct democracy. Let us explore some of these briefly. First, it is sometimes argued that citizens are not qualified, or not sufficiently competent, to deal with complex policy questions. There is no definitive answer to this question, but in reply one might say that elected representatives are not necessarily vastly more competent than ordinary citizens (especially with imaginative use of, for example, special deliberative forums such as citizens' juries). Elected representatives in strong party systems are themselves prevented from exercising any real degree of independent judgement. Besides, one might ask, is there ever a neutral body of experts that fully understands complex problems and agrees on their solution (e.g., effects of radiation)? Perhaps direct democracy can even bring *more* expertise to bear on complex questions? And, as Budge points out, are not citizens better informed, or do they at least have more ready access to information, now, in the information age? ·

Second, it is sometimes suggested that direct democracy would result in minority groups being swamped by intolerant populist majorities. In reply, one can say that direct democracy does not mean that citizens, especially vulnerable minority citizens, should lose their basic rights. Courts in the United States, where the referendum operates in approximately two-thirds of the states, are not slow to strike down laws passed by referendum if they judge that people's rights have been undermined.

Third, direct democracy does not escape certain logical problems of voting. Indeed, some see it as especially vulnerable to these problems. The difficulty, in essence, is that there is no neutral or reliable way to find out the 'will of the people'. To some extent, all electoral and voting systems are arbitrary, in the sense that the outcomes depend in part on the specific shape of the procedure that produced it. Putting it more precisely, it has been shown that where there are three or more voters and three or more candidates for election (or options in a referendum), there may be no avoiding 'cycles', whereby each candidate can be beaten by another candidate, and there is no 'majority' winner (McLean 1986; Budge 2000). Some commentators have seen voting cycles as a decisive problem against direct democracy – how can a genuine majority choice be found, given these logical problems? But why is it more of a problem for direct than representative democracy? We still vote for representatives, and, as far as we know, our votes may often be cyclical (most of the time we don't know, because in order to know we would need to know most voters' order of preferences for all candidates or options). Cycles can in part be avoided by party ideologies bringing policy issues into line along one 'dimension' – the left–right dimension. Once that happens, it is logically possible always to locate a majority winner on that dimension. Budge's innovation is to point out that, in a system with extensive use of referendums for deciding policy issues, parties would be no less involved than they are in more familiar representative systems.

Fourth, is direct democracy open to manipulation by special interests and demagogues? This is a common charge in the United States. But on the other hand, current political processes in representative systems, built around spin and news management, can themselves be highly manipulative. Insofar as upcoming referendums provoke public debate on the issues, then perhaps that debate will tend to act as a guard against troubling levels of manipulation. Finally, there is the argument that direct democracy undermines representative government. But surely it need not do so. Much will depend on the context, the extent to which democracy is widely accepted and defended, and so forth. It could just as readily work the other way around: direct democracy can bolster the legitimacy of representative systems. The two do not constitute mutually exclusive alternatives, but rather complementary devices.

Cosmopolitan democracy

David Held (1995) influentially contends that the future health of democracy depends upon the entrenchment and defence of a common set of democratic rights and obligations at local, national, regional and global levels. A move towards cosmopolitan democracy could deepen the capacity of people affected by decisions and actions which increasingly escape nation-state control to have a say in them. The rights concerned – based on the principle of autonomy – range from civil and political through to cultural and reproductive rights. In institutional terms, Held envisages effective new courts and parliaments operating at regional and global levels, entrenching and enacting these rights and opportunities as part of a 'common structure of political action'.

The issues Held addresses are both basic and complex. For political or economic developments which have a significant impact on populations across a number of countries, how can democratic consent – and with it democratic legitimacy – be attained without a democratically constituted supra-national political entity? How can the 'democratic deficit' of virtually all international political institutions be addressed effectively if not by extending and adapting democratic rights, principles and institutions to levels of governance beyond the national?

Held innovates along dimensions [A] and [B] in particular. With respect to the issue of political community, cosmopolitans argue that democracy ought not to be understood primarily as being applicable above all to nation-states, but also and equally at other levels from the local to the global. With regard to majority rule and citizen rights, democratic majorities at any level must be constrained from transgressing a wide array of autonomy rights. The (underdeveloped) cosmopolitan view of nested layers of legislatures and courts from the local to the global also offers a distinctive perspective on federalism (Held writes of his cosmopolitan model as involving something 'between the principles of federalism and confederalism'; 1995, 230). Certainly it is interesting to think of these concepts as applicable to more than simply national contexts, and so outlining a case for this model being innovative with regard to our dimension [C] as well.

How compelling are these cosmopolitan breaks with the 'default mode'? Even setting aside dispute over the nature and extent of 'globalization', some question whether democratic citizenship can ever operate in any conventional way above the national level (Kymlicka 1999; Wendt 1999). Others go further, such as Robert A. Dahl, who argues that 'an international organization is not and probably cannot be a democracy' (Dahl 1999, 19). According to Dahl, if we consider that international organizations and processes operate on such a scale; with such remoteness from ordinary people's lives; with respect to issues whose complexity evades the vast majority; and in a context where the diversity of peoples and nations makes common interests elusive at best, then we can only conclude that cosmopolitan models tend to be over-optimistic.

If Held's innovation on the first dimension is hotly disputed, on the second it is hardly any less so. There are issues arising from the sheer range of rights Held argues ought to be constitutionalized (or taken out of majoritarian hands). It is true that there is no *inherent* tension between democracy and constitutional limits on what majorities may decide (Saward 1998, chapter 3). But if the set of democratic rights extends far beyond familiar civil and political rights, such as rights to freedom of speech and to a vote of equal value, we can find ourselves on a 'slippery slope' where the courts must resolve issues that arguably belong in the realm of 'normal' democratic politics. In short, the cosmopolitan model appears to shift the balance between constitutionalism and democracy in favour of the former.

In addition, some of the specific rights Held proposes for constitutionalization might prove to be especially controversial, such as suggested rights to 'control over fertility' and to a 'guaranteed minimum income'. Although Held argues that such rights ought to be enacted in ways that are 'sensitive to the traditions, values and levels of development of particular societies' (Held 1995, 201), there appears to be some slippage between the need for a 'common structure of political action' (built on common rights) and any *particular* common structure. Arguably, a common structure of action on a regional or global scale would (a) need to be 'thinner' or more minimalist than Held appears to suggest, and (b) concerned more with procedures and less with substance.

Often enough, disputes *within* one of democracy's key dimensions spill over into disputes about others, or about their relative importance. Dryzek (2000) argues that Held's four nested layers of political units, with their array of familiar governmental institutions and overlapping jurisdictions, are less than adequate in that they *replicate* conventional nation-state models – formal government of continuous territorial units within specific physical borders. In his view, state-like structures are too inflexible; transnational democratization must depend more on transnational *civil society* (in part addressing issues in dimension [A] by subordinating them to issues in dimension [F]). For Dryzek, 'discursive democracy' in informal or non-state cross-border networks represents the future of democratization in the transnational sphere. Dennis Thompson is likewise critical of Held's model, partly for the ways in which he thinks its dispersal of political authority will render accountability more elusive and complex (a point of relevance to dimension [E]), but also because it does not take the idea of deliberative democracy sufficiently on board. It is difficult to know how to organize cross-border votes; it is easier (arguably) to organize cross-border talk or deliberation on issues of mutual concern. Thompson thinks international accountability and decision-making can be enhanced if, for instance, 'a state could establish forums in which representatives could speak for the ordinary citizens of foreign states, presenting their claims and responding to counter-claims of representatives of the host state' – 'a kind of Tribune for non-citizens' (1999, 121–2).

We can glimpse how the cosmopolitan model has begun to shift the focus of political theory on dimension [A] especially. Its critics largely accept that the problems it seeks to address are real ones. At the same time, one does not have to accept a strong version of the globalization thesis to see cosmopolitan democracy as a compelling vision. It is difficult to envisage transnational democratic forms not continuing to develop, however haltingly; or the motivations behind cosmopolitan models subsiding. But perhaps the *type* of democracy that evolves in this context will be something produced from a different mould than Held suggests – transforming our ideas of what counts as 'democracy' along the way. If, for example, Dahl (1999) and Hirst (2000) are right to be sceptical about whether democracy in any conventional sense can work at that level, then perhaps democracy will (have to) mean forms of reason-giving accountability rather than constituencies voting; official-to-official and official-to-group rather than representative-to-electorate accountability.

Ecological democracy

Political ecologists do not offer a new, three-dimensional model of democracy, but rather an orientation towards, and a set of focused criticisms of, democratic orthodoxies. Many of these criticisms resonate with cosmopolitan and deliberative concerns.

Green political theorists, like greens in general, have been highly critical of the idea and practice of representative democracy as we know it (as we saw in the discussion in the previous chapter). Early waves of green political theorizing featured calls for more direct democracy, radical decentralization of political authority to local communities, radical grassroots party organization, and small, rural, face-to-face assemblies on the Athenian model (Bookchin 1982; Sale 1985). Since the early 1980s, though, green political theory has had a more nuanced relationship with democratic norms and practices. Today, the ecological stress is on adapting, renovating and deepening democracy rather than replacing it; rendering it fair and inclusive with respect to non-human interests as well, moving it beyond 'human chauvinism'. Thus, innovation along some of our dimensions of democracy has been a high priority for political ecologists. In particular, this has involved rethinking democratic *procedures*, in line with concern about green attachment to democracy as expressed by Goodin: 'To advocate democracy is to advocate procedures, to advocate environmentalism is to advocate substantive outcomes: what guarantee can we have that the former procedures will yield the latter sorts of outcomes?' (Goodin 1992, 168).

Key ecological emphases arise with respect to dimension [F] – public or private, state or civil society? Suspicious of the extent to which states are locked into ecologically unsustainable economic, military and developmental imperatives, Dryzek favours models of democratization which are more oriented towards and active within civil society; the suggestion here is that democratization (in the West at any rate) has probably gone as far as it can in the formal structures of the state; further democratization (and progress on environmental issues) can and must take place within civil society instead. His examples of such action centre on networks of non-state organizations across national boundaries, targeting, for example, 'biopiracy' in South American rainforests.

With respect to dimension [B], greens have agreed that democracy must be regarded as a self-binding concept. This means that they think democracy needs to limit itself in order to protect itself; majorities cannot do just anything, they cannot legitimately override citizens' rights. But while accepting this view, greens give it a distinctive ecological spin. If majorities must be limited in certain ways for a system to be a genuine democracy, then why can *ecological* limits not be part of a package of constitutional provisions constraining democratic governments? Conceived as a necessary condition for a thriving democratic community, why should not freedom from environmental harm or degradation be analogous to freedom of expression (for example) in the pantheon of democratic thought (Eckersley 1996)?

Further, it has been proposed that familiar representative institutions can and should be adapted so that the vital interests of (in particular) non-human nature and future generations can find a 'voice'. This could work, for example, by the *proxy representation of nature*: interested constituencies (such as memberships of campaigning environmental groups) electing members of parliament whose task is to represent non-human nature, on the grounds that, since democracy is all about representing the interests of the affected, it would be unjust to exclude and thus to discriminate against non-human interests of the natural world (Dobson 1996b). Clearly this idea reinforces the institution of representation and the importance of representative democracy (dimension [D]) by remoulding it. Prior to that – indeed, as a condition of it – fundamental interpretations of what it takes to be a member of a political community are being challenged head-on (a key aspect of dimension [A]). The idea of new, and multiple, communities-of-fate is important here. Environmental circumstances link the destinies of people, animals, and the rest of non-human nature in fateful/inescapable spaces. Boundaries for democracy thus defined are fluid, shifting and unpredictable rather than fixed and securely known over time. And related to this, the meaning and potentialities of accountability (dimension [E]) are radically broadened in green thinking. Accountability to the interests of non-human nature, accountability across the generations, constitutional accountability for the specific circumstances of community thriving – in these and other senses, accountability like representation comes under renewed questioning by green thinkers.

Many of these would-be innovations are linked by green theorists to the ubiquitous deliberative current in democratic thought. According to Eckersley, deliberative approaches can foster a long-term view, and prompt deliberators to hear expressions of, and ideally to take on board, others' (including nature's) interests. It is vital, though, to link representative innovations to deliberation by insisting on the inclusion of the marginalized. Perhaps the most challenging point here is how democratically to include non-human interests in parliamentary and bureaucratic policy-making procedures, if not through Dobson's proxies. Eckersley, for example, advocates a number of innovative mechanisms, including an 'Environmental Defenders Office' and constitutional entrenchment of the 'precautionary principle', which guards against actions which may carry considerable ecological risks (Eckersley 2000). Clearly this complex vision of an ecological democracy calls for innovations across the range of democracy's core dimensions. Some of these innovations involve adapting the familiar – legal rights, for example. Others, such as proxy representation for nature, have a more utopian look. But for how long? In twenty years, given the recent pace of the development of environmental consciousness and awareness, it ought to be no great surprise if the unthinkable has become thinkable – and even seen as necessary.

The politics of presence (and 'difference')

Advocates of a 'politics of presence' (and the related 'politics of difference'), like deliberative democrats, are critical of how liberal democracy has traditionally viewed democratic citizens as fundamentally the same as each other: a citizen is someone with rights and obligations by virtue of membership of the state. No particular characteristics, sexual, ethnic, linguistic, cultural or religious, attach to the category of citizen. Feminist and multicultural critics have challenged this apparently neutral view of citizenship, arguing that it masks processes of social and cultural exclusion and inequality by in turn masking differences that are highly relevant to a more sophisticated view of equal treatment.

For Phillips (1995), a key response to the relative exclusion of (for example) women and ethnic minorities from formal political institutions (such as representative parliaments) in many Western democracies is to supplement 'the politics of ideas' with 'the politics of presence'. Party and parliamentary politics as we are broadly familiar with it, she argues, is about what representatives *do* rather than who they *are*; about the ideas (or policies or ideologies) they press for rather than their gender, race, religion, etc. It is no longer enough, on her view, to lay much greater stress on representing ideas; instead, we should elevate the importance of addressing 'the inclusion of previously excluded voices' by promoting a politics of presence (1995, 10). Parliaments should have a gender, ethnic (and so forth) composition that broadly reflects the population at large. Even if more women and black MPs, for example, do not necessarily represent some mythically essentialist view of 'women's' or 'black' interests, representation, like justice, needs to be seen to be done, as well as to be done (1995, 82).

If Phillips's approach is basically reformist – supporting practical changes that would heighten the presence of previously relatively excluded voices from representative legislatures – that of Iris Young has been more radical (and perhaps more difficult to pin down). Young has stressed the importance of forms of deliberative democracy which take fully on board group difference – indeed she has called her preferred conception 'communicative democracy' and said that this alternative model goes 'beyond deliberative democracy' (Young 1996). Where Phillips is wary of strong guarantees of representation for (e.g.) women in legislatures, Young argues that 'commitment to political equality entails that democratic institutions and practices take measures explicitly to include the representation of social groups whose perspectives would likely be excluded from expression in discussion without those measures' (Young 2000, 148). Her earlier work involved demands that a certain number of seats in the legislature be reserved for members of marginalized groups. She has moved from this position, favouring the principle but being more flexible about the means of achieving it – forms of proportional representation in multi-member constituencies, for example, would avoid tendencies to 'freeze' the characters of groups into false essences (Young 2000, 148–53).

'Difference' and 'presence' theories challenge democratic orthodoxy across the six dimensions, in ways that variously reinforce and diverge from cosmopolitan and deliberative critiques. They stress the ways in which populations of contemporary Western states at least are highly differentiated and varied in cultural and other ways; social and cultural pluralism, not homogeneity, is the challenge that models of democracy must confront [A]. On the second dimension [B], some 'difference' logic would add group rights, perhaps even group vetoes, to the 'list' of constitutional limits on what democratic majorities may do. That is a controversial move: individualism and individual rights have been powerful underpinnings for the idea of democracy throughout the modern period, notwithstanding the importance of groups (such as trade unions) in fighting for the achievement and deepening of democracy, historically. But perhaps democracy today does demand radical redress for long marginalized interests, and perhaps too the strength of that demand in the principle of equality lends it democratic credibility despite its anti-majoritarian character?

Ideas about rethinking representation among 'difference' democrats have a clear impact upon the shift in emphasis from territorial/federal forms of sub-group autonomy to 'identity' groups [C]; curiously, too, they shore up representative rather than direct forms of democracy by (as these theorists see it) adapting the concept of 'representation' itself [D]. With regard to accountability [E], they press us to make a double adaptation of democratic orthodoxy. First, the deliberative approach of emphasizing accountability as the continuous giving of reasons rather than the existence of formal, hierarchical lines of answerability is adopted; and second, this is deepened by adding the idea of intra-group accountability whereby (for instance) black representatives may be required to justify their actions to black constituencies within a larger system of group representation. By the same token, these approaches could be said to offer ways in which key divisions and social inequalities in civil society may be addressed by revising democratic structures in the state [F].

For a mid-range theory, the 'politics of presence' highlights pressing challenges to democratic orthodoxy in diverse, multicultural, multifaith societies, such as France, the UK and the USA. Controversy attends ways in which political representation might need to be reshaped to reflect the demands of 'presence'. One can expect institutional innovations here to continue, by necessity.

Associative democracy

Visions of associative democracy, most notably in the work of Hirst (1994) and Cohen and Rogers (1992), continue to be highly influential among political theorists and policy-makers looking for new, diverse and flexible ways to make and deliver policies in the wake of a broad loss of confidence in, and political and philosophical support for, the traditional top-down model of the welfare state. Proponents of ideas of associative democracy look to move beyond the individualist–statist divide (in theory and in practice) to make voluntary groups or associations the focal point for the citizen's participation in, and engagement with, his or her community. As such, they stress new forms of responsibility and accountability at the local level, reducing the role of the central state. Association-alists seek a 'dispersed, decentralized democracy' which 'combines the individual choice of liberalism with the public provision of collectivism' (Hirst 1994, 189; 22).

In Hirst's associative democracy, which I take as the base-line, the existing structures of liberal democracy would be supplemented (and in some cases replaced) by a range of new institutions, mostly local associations such as religious and cultural organizations, interest groups and trade unions. Publicly funded according to a formula reflecting the quality, coverage and character of their provisions, these associations would take over much of the delivery – and up to a point also the devising – of welfare services. In principle, citizens would be free to opt in and out of associations (and their services) as they wish. The context for this decentralized, pluralistic associationalism would be an economy which has a much more local and regional focus and in which small and medium-sized firms would take on an array of public functions, perhaps most crucially welfare service delivery. In this vision, the role of the state would change quite dramatically, from a provider to an enabler or facilitator of services as well as a standard-setter for more decentralized systems.[3]

Associative visions offer innovations on a number of the core dimensions of democracy. While the nation-state as the territorial basis of a democratic community is not questioned in any substantial way within this model (dimension [A]), clearly the role and status of democratic majoritarianism *is* (dimension [B]). Here, the restrictions on democratic majorities are couched not in terms of constitutional rights, but rather in terms of a radical decentralization of political power such that central government majorities can have little impact on on-the-ground political change. So, the associative model encourages us to remodel our basic interpretations of dimension [B]. It ought no longer be conceived as a continuum from majoritarianism to constitutionalism. Instead, it raises questions about the nature and extent of central government's legitimate role vis-à-vis local associative provision. Associationalists and their critics debate whether traditional majoritarianism might be bypassed entirely, in favour of the local community and group-centred system of regulation and decision-making – reminding us in the process that it is the individualistic basis of democratic theory that makes majoritarianism a central category, and that that basis is in the end optional. Strong forms of association or group-based pluralism can contribute to paradigms in which (a) the very idea of majority rule makes little sense, but (b) the depth of democratic choice and welfare is, arguably, increased.[4]

Associative democracy clearly envisages a significant shift in focus from territorial to functional sub-groups (dimension [C]), though the confederal vision favoured by Hirst combines territorial and functional modes of representation. It is not clear how a working associative order would resolve inevitable tensions between the claims to legitimacy and domains of activity (such as general standard-setting for service delivery) represented by institutions based on these two modes respectively.

With respect to the representative–direct divide (dimension [D]), associative democracy adopts and radically modifies elements of both in a new structure of representation and participation. The 'direct' element is exercised not (primarily, at any rate) through voting, but rather via participation in and through associational life of regions and localities. 'Representation' goes beyond a traditional electoral-constituency basis; one's needs are represented through associations which gain or lose materially according to how well they are perceived to serve the relevant interests. Similarly, democratic accountability takes on a different meaning (dimension [E]), involving the accountability of local associations both to their members and recipients of their local services, and to central government with respect to maintaining basic framework, minimum standards for service-delivery. Significant emphasis is placed upon self-determination at the local level in civil society as an alternative to state provision and determination of services (dimension [F]) – activating the participative potential of civil society is close to the heart of associative visions. In short, on various dimensions, the associative model rethinks the meanings of basic democratic concepts and practices.

Conclusion

This chapter has covered enormous ground in a short space. I hope enough has been said to show that the major challenges confronting democracy are finding answers. I hope also that it shows that those answers are not decisive and finished, and that the debate about democracy's futures remains as open and lively as it is important.

Conclusion

The normal job for a conclusion is to reiterate, or perhaps reveal, the book's 'answer'. But it will be clear from each chapter of the book that, where democracy is concerned, each possible answer provokes new questions – questions that can only be ignored by restricting the discussion in an artificial way. For example, each of the new (and not so new) innovations that were outlined in chapter 5 provides a rich field for debate about what can and should really count in tomorrow's democracy. Some of them are more ambitious than others, and some have been subject to greater criticism than others. But none represents unambiguously the best future course for democracy.

Of course, other works can be found which advocate particular models of democracy – I have written one myself which, among other things, stresses the democratic credentials of direct democracy (Saward 1998). My task here is different – to provide a selective overview of debates about democracy, with the aim of provoking further thought and discussion rather than channelling it in a particular direction. I hope in the process to have provided some tools for critical thinking about democracy, and about politics more generally, for students and general readers.

Each chapter explored the idea of democracy with these points in mind. In the opening chapter I resolutely delayed defining democracy in precise terms. Perhaps that seemed an odd way to open a textbook on democracy. Students in particular often want to know, straight off, what these concepts *really* mean. The main problem with saying too quickly what democracy 'really' means is that it discourages critical thinking about the meanings, connotations and varied uses of such terms. It is true that single definitions can act as 'anchors' for our thinking, and this can be a good thing. But sometimes anchors can also hold us down, preventing us from finding different possibilities. We have looked at a range of real-world and hypothetical examples, which threw up a diverse set of meanings and values for democracy. If there was an essential message in the analysis in chapter 1, it was that democracy is not just a political idea, it is a *living* political idea. And its domain is the life of politics, not a detached world of dictionary entry writers.

The world of democracy is not one of chaos, however. In chapters 2 and 3 we saw how key narratives or stories about democracy have been constructed, focusing on key twentieth-century narratives. These accounts of democracy have indeed anchored much of the thinking about democracy in recent decades. I suggested that the dominant narrative was 'Schumpeterian' – built on the 'competitive elite' assumptions at the core of Joseph Schumpeter's work in the 1940s. It was also clear that there is considerable variation within this dominant narrative; through certain texts by writers such as Downs, Dahl and Lijphart, the narrative changed shape and emphasis without losing its essential character. Equally clear was the fact that this dominant narrative was contested on a variety of levels by counter-narratives, notably participative, Marxist and feminist ones. It would be a mistake to suggest that the differences between these different conceptions are hard and fast – even radical participationists largely accept the necessity of competitive, representative democracy at the national level, for example.

Economic, social and technological change can undermine the conditions for familiar conceptions of democracy, and create challenges that democracy must overcome if it is to thrive. These challenges are constant, and various. In chapter 4 we looked at a small but significant sample of such challenges, in particular globalization and environmentalism.

Each of these developments – themselves disputed widely as far as their basic character is concerned – has radically altered some of the fundamental assumptions of democracy, such as the relation between people and non-human nature, and the status of the nation-state as the basis of democracy's subject population. In both of these cases, it is too early to see what the continuing impact on democracy will be; but it is clear enough that it will be substantial.

Certainly it appears that the apparent triumph of democracy has been accompanied by especially intense debate about its meaning, value and realization. The nature of that debate reflects the extent of challenges such as those of globalization and the demands of environmental sustainability. In chapter 5 I canvassed some of the main recent responses to democracy's challenges. But the six innovative models or conceptions discussed there did not simply adapt the familiar narratives sketched in earlier chapters. In some cases at least, the very assumptions that those familiar narratives were based on were overturned – for instance, the primary role of the state in the view of associative democrats. I noted at the beginning of chapter 5 how the dominant twentieth-century narratives of democracy stood with respect to six key dimensions of democracy. This enabled us to see just how innovative some recent work was – and indeed areas that were left untouched in new conceptions.

What will democracy look like in the future? In the midst of the present phase of debate and potential reinvention, we cannot see at all clearly its destination – the model of democracy, perhaps radically different from today's variants, that may emerge. But we might conjecture at this point that many of its core elements may be products of trends and ideas discussed in this book, including:

- counter-intuitive thinking in political ecology, which, for example, may make the political representation of non-human interests perfectly thinkable;
- the detachment of democracy from the nation-state and other territorial ways of thinking about political communities;
- the importance of talk, deliberation and reason-giving to shaping government, not excluding the importance of

voting and elections but perhaps displacing them up to a point.

These possibilities emerge from present trends, the end-point of which is radically unclear. Many of them pull in different directions, of course. That is nothing less than we would expect, having seen how the idea of democracy has developed. As it was pointed out in the Introduction, the job of building democracy is never done.

Glossary: Conceptions of Democracy

Democracy is a general concept, but there are many particular conceptions or versions of it. The following list sets out a variety of conceptions that feature in debates about democracy more broadly, from ones which refer to a whole political system (e.g., ancient democracy) to others which pinpoint desirable features of democratic systems (e.g., ecological or green democracy). We encountered most of these conceptions in the book; this list is no substitute for those fuller discussions. It is worth stressing the point that lists such as this tend to disguise the sheer diversity of origin and reference that the entries cover. However, it is helpful sometimes to have side-by-side snapshots.

The list is selective, not exhaustive. Indeed, readers might look out for conceptions not included here, especially newer twenty-first-century ones, and think about how they relate to previous conceptions. Further, the suggested meanings are indicative rather than definitive. They are not meant to be read as formal dictionary definitions (we saw in chapter 1 how efforts to 'fence off' particular meanings for such rich concepts are likely to fail).

One (and occasionally two) sources are provided for most entries, including references to chapters in this book, for readers to follow up. Full publication details for these sources can be found in the bibliography.

African democracy A conception emphasizing communal deliberation and discussion, usually face to face, until a group consensus is reached. Prominent in sub-Saharan Africa in the 1960s as many countries gained independence, it was claimed to be distinct from 'Western' democracy – community, consensus, unity and one-party states for 'Africa' versus individualism, pluralism, conflict and multi-partyism for 'the West'. Allegedly rooted in indigenous African political tradition. (See Nursey-Bray 1983.)

aggregative democracy A contemporary label applied to collective decision-making by voting or the 'counting of heads'. Often used pejoratively by advocates of *deliberative democracy* who prefer to highlight deliberation or discussion rather than aggregation or voting. Critics have pointed out how deliberative democracy also relies on voting, suggesting that the divide is more apparent than real. (See Saward 2001.)

ancient democracy A version of face-to-face *direct* or *assembly democracy* as practised in Greek city-states from around 2500BC. Community decisions were made by the votes of the assembled citizens. In reality only a minority could participate in politics – women, foreigners and slaves, for example, were excluded from citizenship. Widely regarded as the first form of democracy historically, especially in its famous incarnation in ancient Athens. (See Dunn 1992.)

Asian democracy A late twentieth-century conception derived from the style of government of Singapore in particular, but also practised for a time in Taiwan and South Korea. It is based around the idea of the one-party state, with a stress on consensus, obeying moral leadership, the claims of the community rather than the individual, and personal discipline. Most prominently articulated by former Singapore Prime Minister Lee Kuan Yew. Critics allege that the idea is semi-democratic at best.

assembly democracy Direct, face-to-face decision-making by a community's members gathered together. Less often taken to refer to a community's *representatives* deliberating and deciding matters collectively. Most noted in ancient Greece (see ancient democracy), but practised in modern Switzerland. (See Hansen 1991.)

associative democracy A contemporary conception emphasizing the importance of informal and local associations performing governance functions on behalf of their members. It represents a decentralized vision opposed to more than a regulatory function for the central state; decisions on (for example) health and education services should be *local* ones. Linked to pluralist democracy in its preference for multiple and diverse centres of power. (See Hirst 1994; chapter 5 above.)

audience democracy A label applied as part of an argument that contemporary democratic systems are dominated by media images rather than policy substance. According to those who use the label, audience democracy's fluidity of policy change contrasts with the policy and ideological stability of the era of *'party democracy'*. (See Manin 1997.)

Christian democracy An ideology as well as a conception of democracy. Generally conservative, it has emphasized the importance of social groups such as the family to the cohesion of societies. Opposed to both unregulated markets and strong states, it has been a pragmatic ideology of government. Christian democracy is the guiding ideology of many mainstream right-wing parties in Western and other democratic systems, including, for example, the German CDU.

communicative democracy A contemporary variant of *deliberative democracy*, stressing deliberation across the gaps of misunderstanding and perspective that divide culturally diverse groups. Now largely absorbed under the deliberative label. (See Young 1996.)

competitive elite democracy The dominant twentieth-century conception, which understands democracy as competition between elites via political parties in elections. In its original form it viewed ordinary citizens as largely incapable of political rationality, and therefore downplayed the desirability of their participation in politics beyond occasional voting. (See Schumpeter [1943] 1976; chapter 2 above.)

cosmopolitan democracy A contemporary conception advocating the practice of democracy in and among institutions operating above the level of the nation-state, e.g., through regional parliaments and executives like those of the

European Union, or a proposed 'world parliament'. Also features the development of international law to which states are subject. (See Held 1995; chapter 5 above.)

delegative democracy A form of democracy said to be characteristic of certain countries which underwent initial transitions to democracy from authoritarianism from the 1980s. It is *electoral democracy* but not, it is argued, fully *representative democracy*, since elected leaders are free to act as they wish constrained only by realities of power relations. A form of democratic government which as yet lacks the institutions and consolidation to be called a fully democratic regime. (See O'Donnell 1994.)

deliberative democracy A conception of democracy which emphasizes the importance of talk, discussion and debate to democratic practice, rather than voting. Advocates argue that deliberation improves the quality and acceptability of collective decisions. Varieties of deliberative democracy range from an emphasis on microcosmic representation to enhanced deliberation in representative legislatures. (See Saward 2000; chapter 5 above.)

developmental democracy A contemporary label for a conception associated with the eighteenth- and nineteenth-century theories of Rousseau and John Stuart Mill, stressing democracy's role in fostering citizens' capacities and their sense of efficacy. (See MacPherson 1977; Held 1996.)

direct democracy A system in which collective decisions are made directly by the people, either by face to face meetings or in *referendums*. In its *assembly* or *ancient* variant, this was the original form of historical democracy. Most often used in twentieth-century and contemporary variants to refer to referendum votes, especially those that are binding rather than merely advisory. (See Budge 1996; chapters 3 and 5 above.)

discursive democracy A variant of deliberative democracy which emphasizes the democratic importance of groups and movements in civil society offering vigorous opposition to (a static and compromised) state power within and across national boundaries. (See Dryzek 2000.)

ecological democracy (also **green democracy**) A contemporary conception emphasizing either (a) decentralized, rural, local, democracy in self-reliant communities living in tune with the natural environment, or (b) a variant of *liberal* or *representative democracy* in which new institutions are designed to ensure representation of the interests of non-human nature and future generations. (See Doherty and de Geus 1996; chapters 4 and 5 above.)

electoral democracy A modern and contemporary conception which underlines the importance of voting in elections for representatives to the theory and practice of modern democracy. It thus de-emphasizes, openly or implicitly, for example, *deliberative democracy*, with its stress on discussion rather than voting, though this is a matter of degree as the bulk of modern conceptions of democracy incorporate the electoral mechanism. (See Sartori 1987.)

industrial democracy A twentieth-century conception emphasizing decision-making by workers within firms, or at a minimum worker participation in aspects of the management of firms or company decision-making. Also encompasses a variety of related schemes, including, for example, the legal rights of workers to be consulted with respect to investment and other company decisions, and worker share-ownership arrangements. (See Dahl 1985.)

juridical democracy A twentieth-century conception emphasizing formal and legal aspects of national democratic decision-making. Advocates argued that in a democracy representatives or legislators should have autonomy (or a 'buffer') from the variety of interest-group pressures which they face, in order to be able to reach transparent and defensible decisions in the common good. (See Lowi 1974.)

liberal democracy A modern and contemporary conception of democracy which emphasizes the liberal focus on constitutional guarantees of individual freedom and rights, among them rights to equality of voting power. In close conjunction with *competitive elite democracy* and *representative democracy*, it is so prominent as an ideal and a practice that it is often used as a synonym for 'democracy' itself. Depending on which of its features are highlighted, its opponent conceptions include *direct democracy, ancient democracy, people's democracy* and *deliberative democracy.* (See Dahl 1989.)

participatory democracy Any form of democracy which emphasizes or enables extensive participation in decision-making by members of the whole group concerned. It may be understood as a national-level conception, for example, in the form of national-level *referendum democracy*, but more often refers to enhanced forms of participation in local communities, the workplace, and within political parties and pressure groups. (See Pateman 1970; Held and Pollitt 1986.)

party democracy A modern and contemporary conception which lays emphasis upon the necessary role of political parties to the ideal and to the practice of democracy. It has also been used as a descriptive label for the period of party-dominated democracy dating approximately from the late nineteenth century to the mid-twentieth century. In the latter sense, it is said to have preceded a current period of *'audience' democracy.* (See Budge 2000; Manin 1997.)

people's democracy A modern conception used to describe the (largely non-democratic) systems of the former Soviet and Chinese blocs of communist countries. It was regarded as opposed to *liberal* (or 'capitalist' or 'bourgeois' or *competitive elite*) democracy, in that it shunned pluralism and conflict in favour of one party representing the 'true' or 'real' interests of the people. (See MacPherson 1966.)

pluralist democracy A modern and contemporary conception emphasizing the multiplicity of interests, and the multiplicity of interest groups to speak for them, in democratic systems. Its advocates often downplayed the electoral mechanism in favour of regarding the interest-group system as the heart of democratic politics, and accordingly emphasized the informal rather than the formal or constitutional aspects of democracy. (See Dahl 1956.)

polyarchal democracy A contemporary conception which attempts to model the key features of *representative democracy.* Those features centre upon the practice of free and fair elections, equal political rights and access to information. The term 'polyarchy' was coined by Robert A. Dahl in an effort to enable scholars to sidestep some of the more normative or moral concerns provoked by the term 'democracy'. (See Dahl 1989; chapters 2 and 3 above.)

protective democracy A contemporary label for a set of conceptions associated with the classic works of (in particular) John Locke and Jeremy Bentham and James Mill, stressing the function of democracy to protect individuals' rights or choices, not least rights to property and its enjoyment, against the encroachment of both other citizens and the state or government. Closely associated with classical ideas about *liberal democracy*. (See MacPherson 1977; Held 1996.)

radical democracy A general label for conceptions of democracy which either (a) advocate highly decentralized and participative ideals of democracy, or (b) envision democracy as involving major social transformations, for example, in terms of prevailing structures of class or gender. (See Holden 1974.) Could include, for example, some versions of *participatory democracy* and *discursive democracy*.

referendum democracy A form of *direct democracy* in which the people make collective decisions themselves by voting on alternative policies without mediation by elected representatives or others. Increasingly common for major or constitutional decisions in many countries in the twentieth and twenty-first centuries. (See Budge 1996.)

reflective democracy A variant of *deliberative democracy* which stresses the internal or mental reflective side of 'deliberation'. (See Goodin 2002.)

representative democracy A modern and contemporary conception which characterizes any version of democracy which highlights decision-making by the elected representatives of the people. As a general and broadly descriptive label, it overlaps closely with (in particular) *liberal democracy* and *polyarchal democracy*; indeed, some would see these as interchangeable labels.

social democracy An ideology as well as a conception of democracy. As an ideology, it envisions and advocates a political system in which the key role of the modern state is to provide tax-funded welfare services such as health and education to its citizens. Social democracy is the guiding ideology of many social democratic and labour parties in Western and other democratic systems, including the German SPD and the British Labour Party.

statistical democracy A classical and modern conception which holds that accurate representation of the people requires that the characteristics of a group of representatives should reflect statistically the characteristics of the larger population from which it is drawn in terms of age, gender, race, and so on. Advocates often favour random sampling or lottery selection of representatives in order to achieve statistical representation. (See Burnheim 1985; Fishkin 1997.)

virtual democracy (or 'e-democracy') A contemporary conception which promotes or emphasizes the use of new information and communications technologies to enhance citizens' political knowledge, access and input. It gets its name from the suggestion that information technologies can account for citizens' voices and opinions in the deliberations of politicians without their physical presence. Possibilities discussed (and in some cases experimented with) have included 'electronic town meetings' using computers; voting by computer; and interactive aids to information about policy issues. (See Kamarck and Nye 2002.)

A Guide to Further Reading

For readers who would like to know more, there are many sources of provocative and informative material on democracy – and of politics more generally. The following guide is a brief and selective note on how to follow up some of the key themes in this book; it offers starting points for further reading, not final destinations. The guide is organized to pick up on concerns and topics that arose in the book's chapters, including both models of democracy and the styles of analysis which were used. Full publication details of books and articles mentioned here are included in the book's bibliography, which follows. Most books are in print at the time of writing, and will generally be available in university and some other libraries.

First, though, let us stay on a general level. In my view, the best all-round contemporary book on the theory and practice of democracy is *Democracy and its Critics*, by Robert A. Dahl. Dahl's classic text reads like philosophy one minute (exploring the reasons why we might regard each other as equals, and therefore deserving democracy) and political history the next (looking at the development of modern democracy, its key features and differences from ancient democracy). Ten years after *Critics*, Dahl published a shorter book which covered many of the same themes – *On Democracy* – which would be useful for those looking for a quicker read, but *Critics* is the classic. One other general text covering theory and practice of democracy is the two-part work by Giovanni Sartori, *The Theory of Democracy Revisited*. Sartori is less systematic but is interesting for being more openly argumentative than Dahl, with a particular point to push against radical participationists.

These works by Dahl and Sartori taken together provide a marvellous account of democracy's past and present, skewed to arguments and debates over fundamental issues of value and meaning. There are various other texts which are meant to introduce democracy, in which the coverage of topics varies. One introduction to the institutions of democracy, especially those to do with the workings of elections, which also deals with conceptual and theoretical issues, is Helena Catt's *Democracy in Practice*.

Let me now turn to more particular themes as they arise from the chapters above. From chapter 1 there are four areas we might mention:

1 *Defining democracy* An excellent discussion of what is at stake in the definition of democracy is chapter 2 of Jack Lively's *Democracy* from 1975. This can be paired with a much more recent effort, that of the opening chapter of David Beetham's *Democracy and Human Rights*. Each of these is clear and comprehensive, and readers will gain a good sense of the definitional possibilities.

2 *The value or justification of democracy* Dahl's *Democracy and its Critics* provides an excellent discussion of justification. Barry Holden's older *The Nature of Democracy* has a chapter on justifications which provides a helpful set of types of justification, a typology which is built upon in chapters 1 and 2 of Michael Saward's *The Terms of Democracy*. For a superb look back to anguished debates about justification earlier in the twentieth century, see Purcell's *The Crisis of Democracy*.

3 *'Close reading'* Sometimes it is not how many items, or how many pages, you read, but how closely you pay attention to what is happening on the page. In chapter 1 some detailed attention was paid to particular uses of 'democracy'. There are techniques of textual analysis, often gathered under the label 'discourse analysis', which encourage this approach, many of them with political

applications. See, for example, Norman Fairclough's chapter, 'The discourse of New Labour: critical discourse analysis', in *Discourse as Data*, edited by Wetherell, Taylor and Yates. The journal *Discourse and Society* is a useful source of articles in this vein.

4 *'Found items'* Democracy happens around us, is contested and criticized and promoted in arguments and speeches which impinge on our daily lives. Paying attention to daily news in newspapers, magazines and other sources can teach us a great deal about the *life* of democracy as a dynamic political idea. A newspaper is not a substitute for a good book on democratic theory, but the two can be made to work together as we move from theory to practice and back again.

In chapters 2 and 3 we looked at the main twentieth-century narratives of democracy, and stretched back selectively to the historical roots of those narratives. A good deal of the examination was text-based. In many ways there is no substitute for reading the original texts – Schumpeter's *Capitalism, Socialism and Democracy*, for example, is engagingly readable. James Mill's classic 'An essay on government' is short and to the point. Generally speaking (and cutting across some impassioned debates about what makes a 'classic'), the classics are classics for a reason – clarity, readability, precision, originality; the work of John Stuart Mill ('Considerations on representative government'), James Madison (contributions to the *Federalist Papers*) and Jean-Jacques Rousseau (*The Social Contract*) is always worth a look.

Having said that, there *are* good secondary overviews of the historical development of the idea of democracy. C. B. MacPherson's *The Life and Times of Liberal Democracy* provides a commendably brief and readable critique of mainstream theories from Locke to Schumpeter. David Held's *Models of Democracy* sets out a number of models in a helpful schematic manner, building in part on some of MacPherson's categories. One might argue with Held's selection and characterization of the 'models' – deliberative and ecological models, for example, are not included – but that type of argument is itself part of the interest.

The challenges to democracy discussed in chapter 4 can each be explored in much greater depth. '*Globalization*' is one of the most contested terms of our times, and there are many sources for the subject. One useful recent collection is *Global Democracy*, edited by Barry Holden. This includes a number of essays by figures such as David Held and Paul Hirst outlining what is at stake for democracy in the wake of globalization (and disputes over the latter's meaning and importance). The most extended single treatment of globalization and democracy is Held's *Democracy and the Global Order*. Several of the chapters in *Democracy's Edges*, edited by Shapiro and Hacker-Cordon, address this connection in some depth. For really in-depth and challenging aspects of globalization debates more generally, such as what it is and the extent to which 'it' is really happening, readers could compare and contrast the arguments in Held and others, *Global Transformations*, and Hirst and Thompson's *Globalization in Question*.

The topic of *environmentalism* and democracy was subject to heated debate in the 1990s. Key contributions to that debate have been gathered in *Democracy and Green Political Thought*, edited by Brian Doherty and Marius de Geus. For an accessible introduction to green political thinking generally, see Andrew Dobson's *Green Political Thought*. Neil Carter's *The Politics of the Environment* is an accessible overview to policy and electoral aspects of green politics. A prominent recent reassessment of where green political thinking has reached is John Barry's *Rethinking Green Politics*. The journal *Environmental Politics* is an excellent source of accessible articles on all aspects of green politics from different countries and regions.

With respect to democracy's capacity to find fertile soil in different cultures, the question of the relationship between religion and democracy is a huge one. Debate about the links between Islam and democracy has been renewed in some quarters by the events of September 11, 2001. For an accessible start, see the chapter by Nazir Ayubi on Islam and democracy in *Democratization*, edited by David Potter and others. This same book contains accessible accounts of democratic development in different regions and cultures.

On the question of measures of democracy, an excellent source of the issues at stake is David Beetham's essay 'Key principles and indices for a democratic audit', which can be found in *Defining and Measuring Democracy* (edited by Beetham), or in Beetham's *Democracy and Human Rights*. Finally, in chapter 5 we looked at new and innovative ideas about democracy for the future. Clearly enough, the best places to look for more ideas here are the innovative texts themselves – works by the authors Fishkin, Held, Dryzek, Phillips, Hirst, Budge, Dahl and others which were cited in the chapter. Beyond those, discussion of a range of innovations, among them chapters by Fishkin, Dryzek and Budge, is included in *Democratic Innovation*, edited by Michael Saward. *Deliberative Democracy* is the title of two collections of articles on that subject, edited by Jon Elster and by James Bohman and William Rehg respectively. Readers may find more accessible and up-to-date material in Fishkin and Laslett's edited collection, *Debating Deliberative Democracy*.

Democracy and Difference, edited by Seyla Benhabib, is a usefully extensive collection of pieces by prominent democratic theorists on 'difference' along with deliberation and other themes. Direct democracy tends to be shunned by the mainstream in democratic theory – there is an argument why deliberative theorists in particular should pay much more attention to direct democracy in Saward's article 'Making democratic connections' in the journal *Acta Politica*. In addition to Budge's book *The New Challenge of Direct Democracy* and his chapter in *Democratic Innovation*, highly informative discussions of the theory and practice of direct democracy can be found in Thomas Cronin's *Direct Democracy* and Maria Setala's *Referendums and Democratic Government*. *Referendums Around the World*, edited by David Butler and Austin Ranney, contains detailed and clear accounts of referendums in various countries along with conceptual discussion. A recent collection of discussions on associative democracy is *Associative Democracy: the Real Third Way*, edited by Veit Bader and Paul Hirst.

These comments, mostly on *books*, have barely scratched the surface of the good material that is available. Excellent and up-to-date analysis of all aspects of democratic politics can be found in academic journals in political science. I would single out in particular: the *Journal of Democracy* (comparative and electoral focus), *Democratization* (comparative and transitions to democracy the main focus), *Political Studies* (more theoretical and conceptual discussions), *Representation* (short articles on elections and related topics), *Political Quarterly* (discussion of democratic systems and public policy, broadly from the left), *Government and Opposition* (comparative focus), and *Environmental Politics* (green issues and ideas). Challenging philosophical discussions can be found in *Philosophy and Public Affairs* and the *Journal of Political Philosophy*. *Political Studies* (UK) is one of a number of general journals which are nationally based and offer a broad range of cutting-edge research articles on democracy and related topics. Others include the *American Political Science Review* (USA) and the *European Journal of Political Research*.

Notes

Chapter 1 Is *This* Democracy?

1 Interview with General Pervez Musharraf, at
   <http://www.guardian.co.uk/pakistan/Story/0,2763,491716,
   00.html> on 16 June 2001.
2 Quoted at
   <http://www.pak.gov.pk/public/news/news2002/appnews2002/
   app30_april.htm> on 1 May 2002.
3 Press reports alleged widespread fraud and lax monitoring at
   the referendum. Pakistan's major political parties boycotted the
   vote. My approach does not mean to dignify Musharraf's
   efforts, but rather to focus on grey areas regarding the question
   'what is democracy?'
4 Quoted at
   <http://www.pak.gov.pk/public/news/news2002/appnews2002/
   app30_april.htm> on 1 May 2002.
5 Certainly this sort of instability of meaning was grist to the mill
   for Roland Barthes (1974), the most prominent theorist of the
   processes of meaning-making discussed here.
6 The definitions are drawn from the following sources: (1) the
   Oxford English Dictionary; (2) Holden (1974, 8); (3) J. D.
   Barber (1995, viii); (4) Moses Finley, quoted in Watson and
   Barber (1990, 9); (5) Julius Nyerere, quoted in Nursey-Bray
   (1983, 101); and (6) Bobbio (1987, 19). Their origins are not
   central to the discussion at hand.
7 Beetham (1999, chapter 1) argues that *definitions* of democracy
   are often about how much the defining author *values* democ-

racy (though they don't say so). He targets the minimalist definition offered by Joseph Schumpeter in particular, something that is discussed in detail in chapter 2.

Chapter 2 Narrating Democracy I

1 On the idea of intertextuality, see Worton and Still (1990).
2 In the 1950s, the study of politics from a normative or value perspective – for example, the attempt to provide 'democracy' or 'equality' with strong value foundations – was under severe threat. Very senior political theorists working in this tradition worried that political philosophy might be 'dead'. The intellectual running in the social sciences and in philosophy was being made by scholars who believed that objective knowledge was attainable only if values were set aside and only factual propositions that were testable were put forward. Downs's work can be seen as a work in the latter, ascendant, tradition. For an outstanding discussion of the roots of these debates, see Purcell (1973).

Chapter 3 Narrating Democracy II

1 This is a disputed claim. See Manglapus (1987).

Chapter 4 Five Challenges

1 For a discussion of these points, see Bollen (1995).
2 This is how Max Weber famously defined the modern state. See Weber (1991, 82–3).
3 Michael Walzer writes: 'Were I to be invited to visit China and give a seminar on democratic theory, I would explain, as best I could, my own views about the meaning of democracy. But I would try to avoid the missioning tone, for my views include the idea that democracy in China will have to be *Chinese* — and my explanatory powers do not reach to what that means . . . the principle of consent requires this much at least: that Chinese democracy be defined by the Chinese themselves in terms of their own history and culture . . . they must make their own claims, their own codifications (a Chinese bill of rights?), and their own interpretive arguments' (1994, 60–1).

Chapter 5   Reinventing Democracy

1   This view is defended most prominently in Gutmann and Thompson (1996, 276–7, especially).

2   In the words of Mansbridge, 'Interest groups, political parties, and social movements, as well as churches, workplaces, ad hoc political collectives, and consciousness-raising groups, provide different forms of protected enclaves, in which members legitimately consider in their deliberations not only what is good for the whole polity but what is good for themselves individually . . . and for their group' (1996, 57). Many of the potential sites for deliberation are discussed in Saward (2000).

3   The associational vision of Cohen and Rogers reflects the structure and concerns of Hirst's in many ways, but is oriented more towards top-down state fostering of appropriate associations for making public decisions and delivering public services; Hirst's vision, however, involves considerably more genuine decentralization and localism.

4   Hirst writes that: 'Majority decisions matter but they have a subsiding part to play in the process of governance. Elections and referenda are relatively infrequent and only decide certain salient issues, whereas governance is a continuous process and all of its decisions cannot be subject to majority approval' (2000, 27).

Bibliography

Aitkenhead, D. (1998) 'We all believe in democracy – er – as long as we get what we want', *The Guardian*, 20 November.

Althusser, L. (1971) 'Ideology and ideological state apparatuses', in Althusser, *Lenin and Philosophy*. London: New Left Books.

Arterton, F. C. (1987) *Teledemocracy*. Beverly Hills, CA: Sage.

Aung San Suu Kyi (1991) *Freedom from Fear and Other Writings*. Harmondsworth: Penguin.

Ayubi, N. (1997) 'Islam and democracy', in *Democratization*, ed. D. Potter et al. Cambridge: Polity.

Bachrach, P. (1967) *The Theory of Democratic Elitism*. Boston: Little, Brown.

Bader, V. and Hirst, P. (2002) *Associative Democracy: the Real Third Way*. London: Frank Cass.

Barber, B. (1984) *Strong Democracy*. Berkeley, CA: University of California Press.

Barber, J. D. (1995) *The Book of Democracy*. Englewood Cliffs, NJ: Prentice Hall.

Barry, J. (1999) *Rethinking Green Politics*. London: Sage.

Barthes, R. (1974) *S/Z*, trans. R. Miller. Oxford: Blackwell.

Beetham, D. (ed.) (1994) *Defining and Measuring Democracy*. London: Sage.

Beetham, D. (1999) *Democracy and Human Rights*. Cambridge: Polity.

Benhabib, S. (1996a) 'Toward a deliberative model of democratic legitimacy', in *Democracy and Difference*, ed. Benhabib. Princeton, NJ: Princeton University Press.

Benhabib, S. (ed.) (1996b) *Democracy and Difference*. Princeton, NJ: Princeton University Press.

Bobbio, N. (1987) *The Future of Democracy*. Cambridge: Polity.

Bohman, J. F. (1998) 'The coming of age of deliberative democracy', *Journal of Political Philosophy*, 6, pp. 399–423.

Bohman, J. F. and Rehg, W. (eds) (1997) *Deliberative Democracy*. Cambridge, MA, and London: MIT Press.

Bollen, K. A. (1995) 'Measures of democracy', in *The Encyclopedia of Democracy*, ed. S. M. Lipset. Washington, DC: Congressional Quarterly; London: Routledge.

Bookchin, M. (1982) *The Ecology of Freedom*. Palo Alto, Cheshire Books.

Budge, I. (1996) *The New Challenge of Direct Democracy*. Cambridge: Polity.

Budge, I. (2000) 'Deliberative democracy versus direct democracy – plus political parties!' in *Democratic Innovation*, ed. M. Saward. London: Routledge.

Burgat, F. and Dowell, W. (1993) *The Islamic Movement in North Africa*. Austin: Centre for Middle Eastern Studies at the University of Texas.

Burnheim, J. (1985) *Is Democracy Possible?* Cambridge: Polity.

Butler, D. and Ranney, A. (eds) (1994) *Referendums around the World*. Basingstoke and London: Macmillan.

Carter, N. (2001) *The Politics of the Environment*. Cambridge: Cambridge University Press.

Catt, H. (1999) *Democracy in Practice*. London and New York: Routledge.

Cerny, P. (1999) 'Globalisation and the erosion of democracy', *European Journal of Political Research*, 36, pp. 1–26.

Cohen, J. (1989) 'Deliberation and democratic legitimacy', in *The Good Polity*, ed. A. Hamlin and P. Pettit. Oxford: Blackwell.

Cohen, J. and Rogers, J. (1992) 'Secondary associations and democratic governance', *Politics and Society*, 20, pp. 393–472.

Combs-Schilling, M. E. (1989) *Sacred Performances*. New York: Columbia University Press.

Cronin, T. E. (1989) *Direct Democracy: The Politics of Initiative, Referendum and Recall*. Cambridge, MA, and London: Harvard University Press.

Dahl, R. A. (1956) *A Preface to Democratic Theory*. Chicago: University of Chicago Press.

Dahl, R. A. (1985) *A Preface to Economic Democracy*. Cambridge: Polity.

Dahl, R. A. (1989) *Democracy and its Critics*. New Haven, CT: Yale University Press.

Dahl, R. A. (1999) 'Can international organizations be democratic? A skeptic's view', in *Democracy's Edges*, ed. I. Shapiro and C. Hacker-Cordon. Cambridge: Cambridge University Press.

Dahl, R. A. (2000) *On Democracy*. New Haven, CT: Yale University Press.

Dalai Lama (1999) 'Buddhism, Asian values, and democracy', *Journal of Democracy*, 10, 1.

Dallmayr, F. (1998) *Alternative Visions: Paths in the Global Village*. Lanham, MD: Rowman & Littlefield.

Dobson, A. (1990) *Green Political Thought*. London: Unwin Hyman.

Dobson, A. (1996a) 'Environmental sustainabilities: an analysis and a typology', *Environmental Politics*, 5, 3.

Dobson, A. (1996b) 'Representative democracy and the environment', in *Democracy and the Environment*, ed. W. M. Lafferty and J. Meadowcroft. Cheltenham: Edward Elgar.

Doherty, B. and de Geus, M. (eds) (1996) *Democracy and Green Political Thought*. London: Routledge.

Downs, A. (1956) *An Economic Theory of Democracy*. New York: Harper & Row.

Dryzek, J. S. (1999) 'Transnational democracy', *Journal of Political Philosophy*, 7, pp. 30–51.

Dryzek, J. S. (2000) *Deliberative Democracy and Beyond*. Oxford: Oxford University Press.

Dunleavy, P. (1991) *Democracy, Bureaucracy and Public Choice*. Hemel Hempstead: Harvester Wheatsheaf.

Dunn, J. (ed.) (1992) *Democracy*. Oxford: Oxford University Press.

Eckersley, R. (1996) 'Greening liberal democracy', in *Democracy and Green Political Thought*, ed. B. Doherty and M. de Geus. London: Routledge.

Eckersley, R. (2000) 'Deliberative democracy, ecological representation and risk: towards a democracy of the affected', in *Democratic Innovation*, ed. M. Saward. London: Routledge.

Edelman, M. (1987) *Constructing the Political Spectacle*. Chicago: University of Chicago Press.

Elster, J. (1988) 'Introduction', in *Constitutionalism and Democracy*, ed. J. Elster and R. Slagstad. New York: Oxford University Press.

Elster, J. (ed.) (1998) *Deliberative Democracy*. Cambridge: Cambridge University Press.

Enayat, H. (1982) *Modern Islamic Political Thought*. London: Macmillan.

Finley, M. I. (1985) *Democracy Ancient and Modern*. London: Hogarth Press.

Fishkin, J. S. (1991) *Democracy and Deliberation*. New Haven, CT, and London: Yale University Press.

Fishkin, J. S. (1997) *The Voice of the People*. New Haven, CT, and London: Yale University Press.

Fishkin, J. S. and Laslett, P. (eds) (2002) *Debating Deliberative Democracy*. Oxford: Blackwell.

Fishkin, J. S. and Luskin, R. (2000) 'The quest for deliberative democracy', in *Democratic Innovation*, ed. M. Saward. London: Routledge.

Goldenberg, Suzanne (1999) 'Coup to "save Pakistan from ruin"', *The Guardian*, 18 October.

Goodin, R. E. (1992) *Green Political Theory*. Cambridge: Polity.

Goodin, R. E. (1996) 'Enfranchising the earth, and its alternatives', *Political Studies*, 44, pp. 835–49.

Goodin, R. E. (2002) *Reflective Democracy*. Oxford: Oxford University Press.

Gramsci, A. (1971) *Selections from Prison Notebooks*. London: Lawrence & Wishart.

Gutmann, A. and Thompson, D. (1996) *Democracy and Disagreement*. Cambridge, MA, and London: Belknap Press.

Habermas, J. (1996) *Between Facts and Norms*. Cambridge: Polity.

Hamlin, A. and Pettit, P. (eds) (1989) *The Good Polity*. Oxford: Blackwell.

Hampsher-Monk, I. (1992) *A History of Modern Political Thought*. Oxford: Blackwell.

Hansen, M. H. (1991) *The Athenian Democracy in the Age of Demosthenes*. Oxford: Blackwell.

Harding, L. and McCarthy, R. (2001) 'Corrupt Bhutto will be put on trial', *The Guardian*, 16 May.

Held, D. (1991) 'Democracy, the nation state and the global system', in *Political Theory Today*, ed. Held. Cambridge: Polity.

Held, D. (1995) *Democracy and the Global Order*. Cambridge: Polity.

Held, D. (1996) *Models of Democracy*, 2nd edn. Cambridge: Polity.

Held, D. and Pollitt, C. (1986) *New Forms of Democracy*. London: Sage.

Held, D., McGrew, A., Goldblatt, D. and Perraton, J. (1999) *Global Transformations*. Cambridge: Polity.

Hertz, N. (2001) 'Why we must stay silent no longer', *The Observer*, 8 April.

Hirst, P. (1994) *Associative Democracy*. Cambridge: Polity; Amherst, MA: University of Massachusetts Press.

Hirst, P. (1997) *From Statism to Pluralism*. London: UCL Press.

Hirst, P. (2000) 'Globalisation, the nation state and political theory', in *Political Theory in Transition*, ed. N. O'Sullivan. London and New York: Routledge.

Hirst, P. and Thompson, G. (1996) *Globalization in Question*, 2nd edn. Cambridge: Polity.

Hobsbawm, E. (2001) 'Democracy can be bad for you', *New Statesman*, 5 March.

Holden, B. (1974) *The Nature of Democracy*. London: Thomas Nelson.

Holden, B. (ed.) (2000) *Global Democracy*. London: Routledge.

Huntington, S. P. (1991) *The Third Wave*. Norman: University of Oaklahoma Press.

Kamarck, E. C. and Nye, J. S., Jr. (eds) (2002) *Governance.com*. Washington, DC: Brookings Institution Press.

Krouse, R. W. (1983) '"Classical" images of democracy in America: Madison and Tocqueville', in *Democratic Theory and Practice*, ed. G. Duncan. Cambridge: Cambridge University Press.

Kymlicka, W. (1999) 'Citizenship in an era of globalization: commentary on Held', in *Democracy's Edges*, ed. I. Shapiro and C. Hacker-Cordon. Cambridge: Cambridge University Press.

Lafferty, W. J. and Meadowcroft, J. (eds) (1996) *Democracy and the Environment*. Cheltenham: Edward Elgar.

Levin, M. (1992) *The Spectre of Democracy*. London: Macmillan.

Lewis, P. G. (1997) 'Theories of democratization and patterns of regime change in Eastern Europe', *Journal of Communist Studies and Transition Politics*, 13, pp. 4–26.

Lijphart, A. (1984) *Democracies*. New Haven, CT, and London: Yale University Press.

Lijphart, A. (1999) *Patterns of Democracy*. New Haven, CT, and London: Yale University Press.

Lindblom, C. (1977) *Politics and Markets*. New York: Basic Books.

Lipset, S. M. (1968) 'Introduction', in R. Michels, *Political Parties*. New York: Free Press.

Lively, J. (1975) *Democracy*. Oxford: Blackwell.

Locke, J. ([1689] 1924) *Two Treatises of Government*. London: J. M. Dent.

Lowi, T. J. (1974) *The End of Liberalism*, 2nd edn. New York: Norton.

McCarthy, R. (2001) 'Pakistan's women get seats at the bottom table', *The Guardian*, 18 May.

McCarthy, R. (2002) 'Musharraf basks in a foregone triumph', *The Guardian*, 1 May.

Macedo, S. (ed.) (1999) *Deliberative Politics*. Oxford: Oxford University Press.

McLean, I. (1986) 'Mechanisms for democracy', in *New Forms of Democracy*, ed. D. Held and C. Pollitt. London: Sage.

McLennan, G. (1990) *Marxism, Pluralism and Beyond*. Cambridge: Polity.

MacPherson, C. B. (1966) *The Real World of Democracy*. Oxford: Oxford University Press.

MacPherson, C. B. (1977) *The Life and Times of Liberal Democracy*. Oxford: Oxford University Press.

Manglapus, R. S. (1987) *Will of the People*. New York and London: Greenwood Press.

Manin, B. (1987) 'On legitimacy and political deliberation', *Political Theory*, 15, pp. 338–68.

Manin, B. (1997) *The Principles of Representative Government*. Cambridge: Cambridge University Press.

Mansbridge, J. (1996) 'Using power/fighting power: the polity', in *Democracy and Difference*, ed. S. Benhabib. Princeton, NJ: Princeton University Press.

Michels, R. ([1915] 1968) *Political Parties*. New York and London: Free Press.

Michels, R. (1949) *First Lectures in Political Sociology*. Minneapolis: University of Minnesota Press.

Miliband, R. (1968) *The State in Capitalist Society*. London: Weidenfeld & Nicolson.

Mill, J. ([1861] 1978) 'An essay on government', in *Utilitarian Logic and Politics*, ed. J. Lively and J. Rees. Oxford: Clarendon Press.

Mill, J. S. (1975) 'Considerations on representative government', in *Three Essays*. Oxford: Oxford University Press.

Nursey-Bray, P. (1983) 'Consensus and community: the theory of African one-party democracy', in *Democratic Theory and Practice*, ed. G. Duncan. Cambridge: Cambridge University Press.

O'Donnell, G. (1994) 'Delegative democracy', *Journal of Democracy*, 5, pp. 55–69.

Pateman, C. (1970) *Participation and Democratic Theory*. Cambridge: Cambridge University Press.

Pateman, C. (1987) 'Feminist critiques of the public/private dichotomy', in *Feminism and Equality*, ed A. Phillips. Oxford: Blackwell.

Phillips, A. (1995) *The Politics of Presence*. Oxford: Oxford University Press.

Pitkin, H. F. (1967) *The Concept of Representation*. Berkeley: University of California Press.

Porritt, J. (1984) *Seeing Green*. Oxford: Blackwell.

Potter, D. et al. (eds) (1997) *Democratization*. Cambridge: Polity.

Poulantzas, N. (1978) *State, Power, Socialism*. London: New Left Books.

Programme of the German Green Party (1983). London: Heretic.

Purcell, E. A. (1973) *The Crisis of Democracy*. Lexington: University Press of Kentucky.

Rousseau, J.-J. ([1762] 1973) *The Social Contract*, trans. D. A. Cass. London: J. M. Dent.

Sale, K. (1985) *Dwellers in the Land*. San Francisco: Sierra Club.
Sartori, G. (1987) *The Theory of Democracy Revisited*, Vol. 1: *The Contemporary Debate*. Chatham, NJ: Chatham House.
Sartori, G. (1987) *The Theory of Democracy Revisited*, Vol. 2: *The Classical Issues*. Chatham, NJ: Chatham House.
Saward, M. (1998) *The Terms of Democracy*. Cambridge: Polity.
Saward, M. (ed.) (2000) *Democratic Innovation*. London: Routledge.
Saward, M. (2001) 'Making democratic connections', *Acta Politica*, 36.
Schaffer, F. (1998) *Democracy in Translation: Understanding Politics in an Unfamiliar Culture*. Ithaca, NY: Cornell University Press.
Schumpeter, J. A. ([1943] 1976) *Capitalism, Socialism and Democracy*, 5th edn. London: Allen & Unwin.
Sen, A. (1999) 'Democracy as a universal value', *Journal of Democracy*, 10, 3.
Setala, M. (1999) *Referendums and Democratic Government*. Basingstoke: Macmillan.
Shapiro, I. and Hacker-Cordon, C. (eds) (1999) *Democracy's Edges*. Cambridge: Cambridge University Press.
Skinner, Q. (1973) 'The empirical theorists of democracy and their critics', *Political Theory*, 1, 3.
Smith, G. (2000) 'Toward deliberative institutions', in *Democratic Innovation*, ed. M. Saward. London: Routledge.
Thompson, D. (1999) 'Democratic theory and global society', *Journal of Political Philosophy*, 7, pp. 111–25.
Toffler, A. and Toffler, H. (1993) 'Societies running at hyper-speed', *The Guardian*, 3 November.
Walcott, H. F. (1995) 'Making a study "more ethnographic"', in *Representation in Ethnography*, ed. J. Van Maanen. London: Sage.
Walzer, M. (1990) 'The communitarian critique of liberalism', *Political Theory*, 18, 1.
Walzer, M. (1994) *Thick and Thin: Moral Argument at Home and Abroad*. Notre Dame, IN: University of Notre Dame Press.
Watson, P. and Barber, B. (1990) *The Struggle for Democracy*. London: W. H. Allen.
Weber, M. (1991) *From Max Weber*, ed. H. H. Gerth and C. Wright Mills. London: Routledge.
Wendt, A. (1999) 'A comment on Held's cosmopolitanism', in *Democracy's Edges*, ed. I. Shapiro and C. Hacker-Cordon. Cambridge: Cambridge University Press.
Wetherell, M., Taylor, S. and Yates, S. J. (eds) (2001) *Discourse as Data*. London: Sage.

Wood, G. S. (1992) 'Democracy and the American revolution', in *Democracy: The Unfinished Journey, 508BC to AD1993*, ed. J. Dunn. Oxford: Oxford University Press.

Worton, M. and Still, J. (eds) (1990) *Intertextuality*. Manchester: Manchester University Press.

Wright, R. (1996) 'Two visions of reformation', *Journal of Democracy*, 7, 2.

Young, I. M. (1996) 'Communication and the other: beyond deliberative democracy', in *Democracy and Difference*, ed. S. Benhabib. Princeton, NJ: Princeton University Press.

Young, I. M. (1997) 'Difference as a resource for democratic communication', in *Deliberative Democracy*, ed. J. Bohman and W. Rehg. Cambridge, MA, and London: MIT Press.

Young, I. M. (2000) *Inclusion and Democracy*. Oxford: Oxford University Press.

Electronic sources

'US elections: is this democracy?', at <http://news.bbc.co.uk/hi/english/talking_point/newsid_1015000/1015061.stm> on 21 November 2000.

'Interview with General Pervez Musharraf', at <http://www.guardian.co.uk/pakistan/Story/0,2763,491716,00.html> on 16 June 2001.

'Referendum to be transparent, fair and impartial', at <http://www.pak.gov.pk/public/news/news2002//appnews2002/app30_april.htm> on 1 May 2002.

Index

accountability
  in cosmopolitan democracy
    131
  as dimension of democracy
    119, 121, 123, 133, 136,
    137
  and representative
    government 61
Afghanistan 5
African democracy 109, 113,
  114, 145
aggregative democracy
  145
Aitkenhead, Decca 30
Algeria 111
al-Qaeda 5
Althusser, Louis 79
Amnesty International 93
ancient democracy 145
anthropocentrism 104–5
Asian democracy 145
assembly democracy 145
associative democracy 137–9,
  146
Athenian democracy 61, 63,
  65, 74–6, 132
audience democracy 146

Bachrach, Peter 67–71
BBC 8
ballot papers, confusing 7
Barber, Benjamin 70, 75
Barry, John 104
Beetham, David 89–90
Belgium 54
Bentham, Jeremy 58–60, 64
bio-piracy 28, 132
'bioregionalism' 107
Bohman, James 122
British Democracy Campaign
  10–12
Buddhism 110
Budge, Ian 124–8
bureaucracy 38
Burke, Kenneth 32
Burma 110
Bush, George W. 7, 93, 95

Cerny, Philip 96
Christian democracy 146
Churchill, Winston 27
'classical' theory of democracy
  38, 67–8
Climate Change Convention
  (Kyoto) 93, 95, 107

Cold War 43, 95
communicative democracy 146
competitive elitism *see*
   Schumpeterianism
complexity
   implications of state 100–1
   policy networks and 102
   types of state 99–100
'consensus' democracy
   features of 53–4
   as majoritarian 55
consent 78, 96–7
Conservative Party (UK) 10
constitutions and
   constitutionalism 21, 126,
   130, 136
contract theory 62
cosmopolitan democracy
   128–31, 146–7
Council of Ministers 55
'country X' 19
coups, military 3
culture and democracy 19, 21,
   23, 108–14
Czech Republic 24

Dahl, Robert A. 47–51, 57,
   79, 96, 101, 129
Dalai Lama 110
Dallmayr, Fred 113
'definitional fallacy', the 46
definitions of democracy
   14–19
   comparing 15
   descriptive 45
   dictionary 15–16
   focus of 17
   necessary components of
     88–9
   operationalizability 40
   sampling and appraising
     14–19
   Schumpeter's 38
   strategies of 17
delegative democracy 147

deliberation and deliberative
   democracy 121–4, 147
   and the common good 113
   cross-border 131
   and group difference 135
   and information 28
   sites for 123–4
   and voting 22
Democratic Audit 90
'democratic deficit' 98, 129
'democratic method', the 38
Democratic Party (US) 70
democratization, 'third wave'
   of 109
'demokaraasi' 112–13
'descriptive method', the 50
designing democracy 19–25
dictatorship 37
difference, politics of 134–7
dimensions of democracy
   116–20
direct democracy 124–8, 147
   and Athenian democracy
     74–6
   and definition of democracy
     17, 65, 71
   ecological visions and 108,
     132
   in Lijphart's model 55
   objections to 126–8
   in participation dimension
     of democracy 118–19,
     122
   party-based model 124–8
   and pyramidal system 70
   and representation 23, 122
   used by Musharraf 5, 6
discursive democracy 122,
   123, 130, 147
discussion, government by 16
Dobson, Andrew 104, 133
Downs, Anthony 43–7
Dryzek, John 122, 123, 130,
   132
dualism, simple 3

'Earth Summit' (UNCED, Rio de Janeiro) 93, 107
Eastern European revolutions 109
Eckersley, Robyn 133, 134
ecocentrism 105
ecological ('green') democracy 131–4, 148
'economic' theory of democracy 43–4
elections
  and claim to represent 64
  electoral turnout 8, 9
  free and fair in polyarchy 49
  as fundamental democratic institution 14
electoral college 7, 9
electoral democracy 148
elite theory, classical 36
empirical models of democracy 54
Enayat, Hamid 111
Engels, Friedrich 77
environmentalism 102–8
  democratization and 132
  electoral and policy impact of 105–6
  and national policy plans 106–7
  radical visions of 107
  spectrum of views 103–5
equality
  broader view of 72
  and citizenship 134
  electoral and social 81
  in Islam 111
  key role in definitions of democracy 18, 88, 90
  and patriarchy 81
  sexual 46
  limits of classical view of 66
  limits of modern view of 66–7
  troubling questions about 7

'eurocommunism' 77
European Commission 55
European single currency 10–12
European Union 10–12, 55, 92, 94–6, 98, 106
extremists and extremism 25

fairness
  key role in definitions of democracy 18
  troubling questions about 7
fascism 37, 38
federalism and federal systems 7, 21, 54, 129
feminist critiques 80–2, 134
Finley, Moses 34, 75–6
Fischer, Joshka 106
Florida 6–9
force, government by 16
freedom of expression 49
French Revolution 60
Friends of the Earth 93, 105
future of democracy 142–3

'general will' 74
Ghannouchi, Rachid 112
global warming 93
globalization
  challenge of 90–8
  and cosmopolitan democracy 131
  impact on democracy 96–8
  and national states 93–6
Goodin, Robert 132
Gore, Al 7
'government (or rule) by the people' 16
Gramsci, Antonio 77–9
'grassroots democracy' 37
Green Party (Germany) 70, 103, 105–7
Greenpeace 93, 105

group autonomy as dimension
of democracy 118
guaranteed minimum income
130

Habermas, Jürgen 123
hegemony 77–8
Held, David 94–5, 128–31
Hertz, Noreena 92, 97
Hirst, Paul 137–9
historical context of democratic
narratives 33–4
human nature and politics
59–60
Huntington, Samuel 109
Hobsbawm, Eric 26–9
hypothetical cases 19–25

ideas
as focus of study of
democracy 34
'politics of', the 135
identity and democracy 10–12,
21
'ideological state apparatuses'
79
India 3, 109
indigenization of democracy
114
individualism 39, 66, 136
industrial democracy 70,
79–80, 148
information technology 91
institutions, mix of 14, 17
interest groups 54
International Monetary Fund
92, 94, 98
intertextuality 34–5, 76
Islam 110, 111, 113
Italy 37

judicial review 54
juridical democracy 148
justification of democracy
27–8

Labour Party (UK) 10, 70
language 19
Latin America 109
Lebanon 24, 111
legislatures 22
leaders and leadership
in classical writings 66
expert and professional 35
as focus of Schumpeterian
model 41
proposed and imposed 40–1
legitimacy and democracy 5
Lenin 78
liberal democracy 120, 148
liberalism 66, 81, 110, 137
liberation movements, 'third
world' 76
Lijphart, Arend 51–6
limiting power 19
Lindblom, Charles 79
Lipset, Seymour Martin 37–8
local politics and democracy 4,
6, 51, 70, 74, 88, 96, 124,
132, 137
Locke, John 62–3

McLennan, Gregor 77
MacPherson, C. B. 67–71, 75
Madison, James 63–4
majoritarian democracy 19–21,
52–6, 138
features of 52–3
and pluralitarian view 55
majority rule 8, 13, 16, 21,
122, 129, 133, 138
Manglapus, Raul 114
Marx, Karl 77
Marxism 76–80
Marxism-Leninism 77
meanings of democracy
connotation 12, 14, 15, 18
as constructed 26, 28, 33,
37, 89
denotation 12, 14, 18
fixing 4, 11

measures of democracy
 dilemmas of 89–90
 in Lijphart 54
 measurability as key to
  definitions 40, 45
 objective and subjective
  indicators 89–90
 in polyarchy 50–1
 threshold and continuum
  86–9
 verifiability 87
media 9
Michels, Robert 35–8, 41
Michelsian dilemma, the 36–8,
 42, 47
Miliband, Ralph 79
Mill, James 60–1
Mill, John Stuart 73–4
'models of democracy'
 cosmopolitan 128–31
 'classical' 58–67
 implies a finished product 32
 non-Western 113, 114
 party-based direct 124–8
 'protective' 62–4
money and politics 8, 9
Mosca, Gaetano 36
Musharraf, General Pervez
 3–6, 12, 88–9
Mussolini, Benito 37

narratives of democracy ix,
 32–3
 core of Schumpeterian 56
 as opposed to models and
  theories 32–3
 realist 38–42
National Health Service (UK)
 70
national (and 'public' and
 'general') interest 6, 9, 13,
 17, 87
'neomedievalism' 96
North Atlantic Treaty
 Organization (NATO) 95

oligarchy, iron law of 35–8
'original democracies' 114

Pakistan 2–6
Palestine 111
Pareto, Vilfredo 36
participation as dimension of
 democracy 118–19
participative democracy 67–76,
 149
 classical roots of 73–4
 local and workplace 51
party democracy 149
Pateman, Carole 67–74, 76
people's democracy 149
Petrella, Riccardo 96
Phillips, Anne 134–7
pluralist democracy 149
policy networks 101–2
political parties 70
political science 45, 46–7, 50,
 67, 101, 109
political unit 14, 17, 23, 26,
 27, 97, 117
polyarchy 47–51
 definition of 149
 institutions of 49
 measurability of
  characteristics 50
 polyarchy II 101
 polyarchy III 102
 'privileged position of
  business' and 79
popular power 17, 18, 22, 88,
 90
Portugal 109
precautionary principle 134
presence, politics of 134–7
property 61
proportional systems 20
protective democracy 62–4,
 65, 150
public and private as
 dimension of democracy
 119–20

public/private dichotomy 81–2
pyramidal system 70

quality of life 100

radical democracy 35, 80,
  107–8, 150
rationality and irrationality
  people's irrational tendencies
    41, 65
  rational political parties 44
  rational voter, the 44
realism 68–9
reasonable interpretation of
    democracy 4, 14, 90
referendums and referendum
    democracy 5, 12, 124–8,
    150
reflective democracy 150
religion 4, 19, 110–12
representation and
    representative democracy
  changing meanings of 63
  definition of 150
  and deliberation 122
  and democratic design
    22–3
  direct democracy and 128
  and Downs's model 45
  of groups 136
  and Lijphart's model 55
  of nature and future
    generations 133
  and participation dimension
    of democracy 118
  through associations 138–9
representatives 18, 127
requirements (or 'demands') of
    democracy 19, 24
rights
  in cosmopolitan democracy
    128, 130
  as dimension of democracy
    117–18
  group 21, 136

minority rights 16, 20, 21,
    136
  to property 62
Rousseau, Jean-Jacques 60, 73

Sale, Kirkpatrick 107
Sartori, Giovanni 42, 75–6
Schaffer, Frederick 112–13
Schumpeter, Joseph 38–42, 45,
    72, 73
Schumpeterianism
  absence of gender in 41–2
  Athenian democracy and
    75–6
  as competitive elitism 146
  core features 38–42, 56
  critics of 67–73
  feminist concerns about
    81–2
  forebears and requisites
    64–7
  link to Downs's model 43
  link to Lijphart's models 54
  Marxist suspicion of 79
  post-Schumpeterian thinking
    42–57
  and protection 62
  and realism 68–9
  summary of participatory
    alternative to 73
  view of leadership 40–1
  view of ordinary people 41
science and technology 98–100
secession 23
self-binding, democracy as
    132
Sen, Amartya 25
Senegal 112–13
September 11, 2001, events of
    4, 95, 111
'sham' democracy 3
Sharif, Nawaz 3
signifiers and signifieds 1–2,
    11–13
social democracy 150–1

society, democratization of
  69–71
Soroush, Abdul Karim 112
South Africa 24
Soviet Union 46, 104
space and belonging as
  dimension of democracy
  117–18
Spain 109
'spin' and news management
  128
standards and criteria for
  democracy 4
'state of nature' 62
statistical democracy 151
sustainability (and sustainable
  development) 103–5, 107,
  132
Suu Kyi, Aung San 110
Switzerland 54

Taliban 5
'teledemocracy' 125
television 91
theory and practice viii–ix
'third world' 7
Thompson, Dennis 130–1
Tibet 110
totalitarianism 37, 46, 69
transnational corporations
  91–2, 94, 97
transparency 88, 90
'true' or 'real' democracy 3,
  5

'ungovernability' 100–1
United Kingdom 10–12, 20
United Nations 92, 94, 98
United States of America
  courts and referendums in
  127

as hegemonic state 95
idea of representation in
  63–4
presidential elections 2000
  6–9
separation of powers 20
utilitarianism 60–1

value of democracy 25–30
and perspective adopted 29
strategic views of 29
as universal 108
virtual democracy (or
  'e-democracy') 151
votes and voting 5, 6, 9, 13,
  22
as critical to democracy 39
logical problems of 127
and technical issues 28
and voice 122

'war on poverty' (US) 70
'war on terror' 4
Weber, Max 36
welfare service delivery 137
women
  exclusion from franchise 61
  exclusion from political
    institutions 134
  guaranteed representation of
    6, 135
Wood, Gordon 63
World Bank 92, 94, 98
World Summit (Johannesburg)
  93, 95, 107
World Trade Organization 91,
  98
World War I 35, 37
World War II 38, 42, 109

Young, Iris 135